Roman Conquests:
Asia Minor, Syria
and Armenia

Roman Conquests: Asia Minor, Syria and Armenia

Richard Evans

Pen & Sword
MILITARY

First published in Great Britain in 2011
and republished in this format in 2022 by
PEN & SWORD MILITARY
an imprint of Pen & Sword Books Ltd
Yorkshire – Philadelphia

ISBN 978-1-39908-521-2

Typeset by Concept, Huddersfield, West Yorkshire, HD4 5JL.
Printed and bound in England by CPI Group (UK) Ltd, Croydon CR0 4YY.

MIX
Paper from
responsible sources
FSC® C013604

Pen & Sword Books Limited incorporates the imprints of Atlas, Archaeology, Aviation,
Discovery, Family History, Fiction, History, Maritime, Military, Military Classics,
Politics, Select, Transport, True Crime, Air World, Frontline Publishing, Leo Cooper,
Remember When, Seaforth Publishing, The Praetorian Press, Wharncliffe Local History,
Wharncliffe Transport, Wharncliffe True Crime, White Owl and After the Battle.

For a complete list of Pen & Sword titles please contact
PEN & SWORD BOOKS LTD
47 Church Street, Barnsley, South Yorkshire, S70 2AS, England
E-mail: enquiries@pen-and-sword.co.uk
Website: www.pen-and-sword.co.uk
or
PEN & SWORD BOOKS
1950 Lawrence Rd, Havertown, PA 19083, USA
E-mail: uspen-and-sword@casematepublishers.com
Website: www.penandswordbooks.com

Contents

Contents

List of Plates

Acknowledgements

First of all I should like to thank Philip Sidnell of Pen & Sword Books for inviting me to put forward my thoughts on the subject of the Roman conquest of the lands east of the Aegean Sea. Moreover, that during the course of this work I have been able, as I intended, to advance new ideas about the wars between the Romans and Antiochus III of Syria, Mithridates VI of Pontus and Tigranes the Great of Armenia, not least concerning the mostly literary sources from which evidence for this study must be gleaned.

In the completion of this project, I should also like to thank Graham Sumner (illustrations), Ian Hughes (maps) and Mike Bishop (editing) for their kind assistance and contributions to the making of this volume, and to all the staff at Pen & Sword for being supportive in this venture. Where inconsistencies or errors remain they are of my own making.

Thanks are moreover due to Cardiff University (School of History, Archaeology & Religion) for providing me with the funds, on two occasions, to visit some of the sites mentioned in this work, including the Hermus Valley and Magnesia-ad-Sipylum. Those visits really brought home to me the geographical extent of Asia Minor (Turkey) and beyond, and hence indeed the magnitude of the struggle between the Romans and their competitors for power and supremacy in this region.

Finally, a word of thanks too to the University of South Africa (UNISA) for its continued interest in my work, for appointing me an Honorary Research Fellow of its Department of Classics and Modern Languages for the last five years, a now-longstanding connection which I certainly hope will endure in the future.

(Pontypridd 2010)

Introduction

The growth of Rome from Italian power to universal empire occupies nearly 250 years; from its acquisition for the first time of overseas territories in Sicily, Sardinia and Corsica between 241 and 238 BC to the subjugation of the Celtiberians in North West Spain and the tribes along the Rivers Rhine and Danube towards the close of the first century. This was an epoch of vibrant acculturation in the Mediterranean as Roman and Greek civilisations blended to bequeath fundamental and pervasive influences on the modern world. This was a time of wars on a scale hitherto unseen, of great Roman triumphs and equally catastrophic disasters. Successfully-concluded wars delivered immense wealth to the Romans who adorned their city to such an extent that it became famed not only during antiquity but has remained a fascination ever since. These same wars paradoxically also created a period of peace – *pax Romana* – which has similarly never been equalled to the present day. This period was one of great innovation and one which produced arguably some of the most influential and dominating figures of world history: Caesar, the elder and younger Cato, Cicero, Pompey, Scipio Africanus. It was also an age, human nature being what it is, of massive corruption and terrible suffering generally excused and condoned as being in the interest of the state. Yet, in tandem, this was also a time of profound religiosity and cultivated lifestyle.

Against this complex and, some might say, weighty backdrop, Rome's conquest of Asia Minor, Syria and Armenia might appear at a cursory glance as a relatively minor event, lacking much controversy or indeed strain on the conqueror. It might almost pass unnoticed. However, this would be a naïve and simplistic take on the events which in fact dominated political agendas at Rome for nearly 150 years. Rome's first contacts with the East came early in its history, with constant exposure to Hellenic influence on account of the close proximity of cities such as Tarentum and Rhegium in *Magna Graecia* and Syracuse in Sicily. The wars for supremacy in the West with Carthage actually drew Rome closer to the East; it was only a matter of time before these worlds collided. Macedonian support for Hannibal in the Second Punic War sparked Roman intervention across the Ionian Sea for the first time, while the intrigues of the Syrian king Antiochus III drew Roman armies across the Aegean. The kingdom of Pergamum was presented to the Roman state in the last will and testament of its king, Attalus, and became the province of Asia. The other kingdoms and states of Asia Minor, Syria too, became Roman provinces or subject states as a result of thirty years of war with Pontus and its great warrior-king, Mithridates Eupator. By the middle of the first century BC Roman might had extended to the mountains of the Caucasus and to the headwaters of the Rivers Euphrates and Tigris. It is this story of conquest which is treated in the following pages.

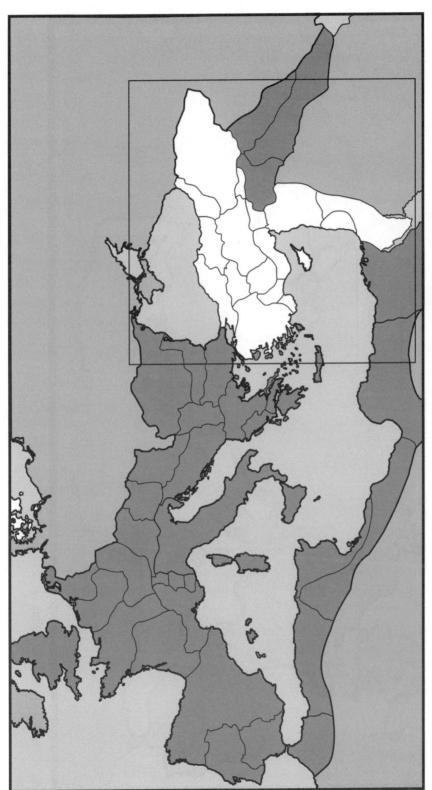

Map 1. The Roman Empire at its greatest extent with the regions covered in the present volume highlighted. (© *Ian Hughes*)

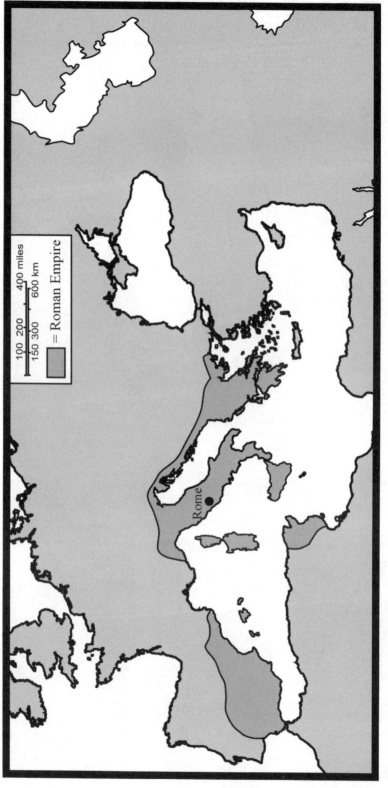

Map 2. The Roman empire in 146 BC. (© *Ian Hughes*)

Scale: 100 200 400 miles / 150 300 600 km

= Roman Empire

Rome

Map 3. Rome's first contact with Greece. (© *Ian Hughes*)

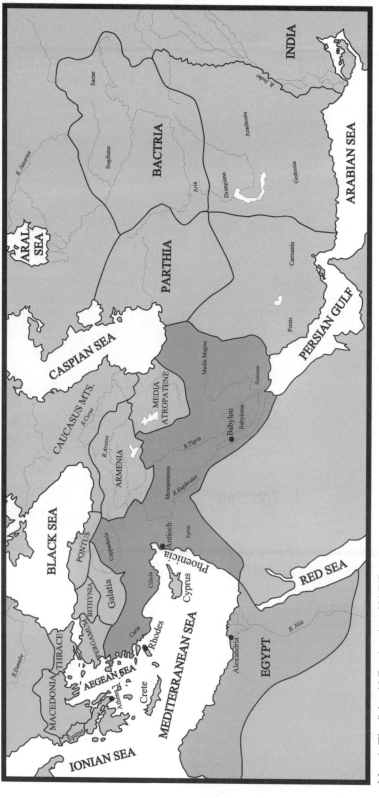

Map 4. The Seleucid Empire circa 200 BC. (© *Ian Hughes*)

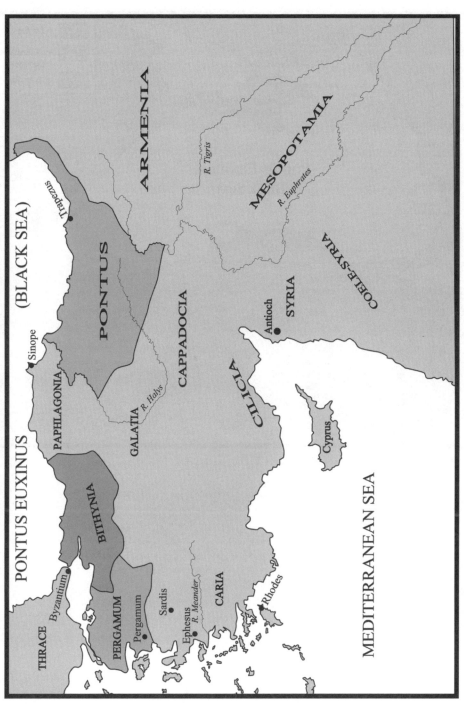

Map 5. Asia Minor. (© *Ian Hughes*)

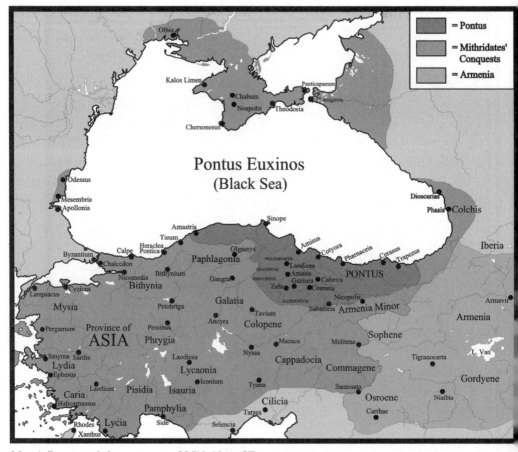

Map 6. Pontus and the conquests of Mithridates VI. (© *Ian Hughes*)

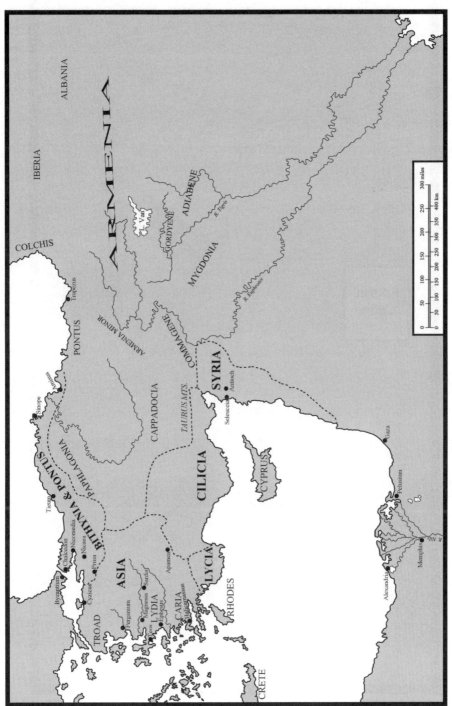

Map 7. Pompey's Settlement of Asia Minor. (© *Ian Hughes*)

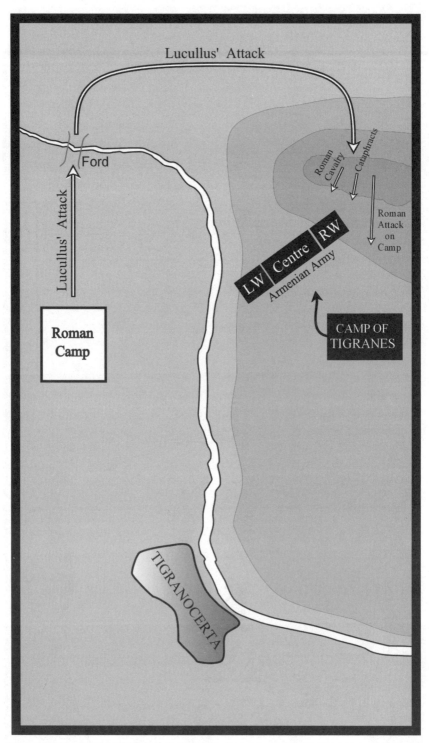

Map 8. Battle of Tigranocerta. (© *Ian Hughes*)

Abbreviations

Standard or easily recognisable abbreviations are used throughout this work. The main ancient sources are abbreviated as follows.

Appian, *Syrian Wars*	App., *Syr.*
Appian, *Mithridatic Wars*	App., *Mith.*
Athenaeus, *The Dinner-time Sophists*	Athenaeus
Cicero, *Oration against Murena*	Cic., *Pro Mur.*
Cicero, *Oration against Verres*	Cic., *Verr.*
Frontinus, *Strategies*	Front., *Str.*
Josephus, *Jewish War*	Josephus, *BJ*
Livy, *History of Rome*	Livy
Pliny the Elder, *Natural History*	Pliny, *NH*
Plutarch, *Life of Aratus*	Plut. *Arat.*
Plutarch, *Life of Cato the Elder*	Plut., *Cato the Elder*
Plutarch, *Life of Lucullus*	Plut., *Luc.*
Plutarch, *Life of Marius*	Plut., *Mar.*
Plutarch, *Life of Pompey*	Plut., *Pomp.*
Plutarch, *Life of Sulla*	Plut., *Sull.*
Polybius' *Histories*	Polyb.,
Strabo, *Geography*	Strabo
Xenophon, *Anabasis*	Xenophon, *Anab.*

All dates are BC unless otherwise stated.

Chapter 1

Roman Interest in Asia Minor and the East

The day of small nations has long passed away.
The day of Empires has come.
(Joseph Chamberlain, 1904)

A casual acquaintance with Roman history and accounts of the acquisition of a world empire might beguile a reader into assuming that the conquest of Asia Minor and Syria was inevitable, and regard it as merely a sequel to earlier Roman triumphs over Carthage and Macedonia. The story of Rome's wars with Carthage is especially dramatic and memorable, and what came after the celebrated defeat of Hannibal may perhaps appear to be predictable and a little dull. The details of Roman involvement in the eastern Mediterranean are, of course, much more complex, the events drawn out over a far longer period, the result much more in doubt than elsewhere, and the question of an eastern frontier never really solved. Besides all these points, the wars of this time produced personalities every bit as intriguing and memorable as those encountered by the Romans in the west. Antiochus III (the Great), king of the Seleucid Empire, Mithridates VI Eupator, king of Pontus, the kings of Pergamum, the Rhodians, the Galatians, leaders of rebellions such as Andriscus and Aristonicus were in all respects worthy adversaries of Rome whose own generals, for instance, Scipio Africanus, Metellus Macedonicus, Cornelius Sulla and Pompey (the Great) were equally dominating figures both at home and abroad. Roman superiority may well have been illustrated on the battlefield and through the portals of high stakes diplomacy, but the attractions of possessing an empire which comprised the heartland of the domain of Alexander the Great nearly proved the undoing of the Romans. Arguably, they were never able to solve the problem of an unstable eastern flank to their empire, a situation which could never be fully consolidated nor the vulnerability to invasion ever overcome. Rome's three wars with Carthage, between 264 and 146 BC, essentially secured the western Mediterranean making it a Latin lake in much the same way that the Tyrrenhian Sea had become 'Mare Nostrum,' and resulted in the destruction of the Phoenician city whose name has become closely associated with trade and religious cults involving child sacrifices.[1] Involvement in the East was, to coin a phrase currently in vogue, of *longue durée* and more hazardous for Rome than elsewhere. It would be quite unwise to assume that since the East was 'more civilized' it was a safer environment than the supposedly more barbaric West. The rulers of states in Asia Minor and of Syria could be quite as ferocious as any Gallic, Germanic or Iberian chieftain or as relentless in pursuit of their ambitions as any Punic, Illyrian or Macedonian leader.

The extremely rash decision of the young Philip V of Macedonia to make himself an ally of Hannibal in the Second Punic War brought him into direct conflict with Rome. From a first encounter with Rome he was able to extricate himself without too much loss. But from a second soon afterwards that culminated in the battle at Cynoscephalae in Thessaly in 197 left him soundly defeated by a Roman army commanded by the consul Titus Quinctius Flamininus. In the subsequent peace treaty his power was severely constrained, and his future status as a 'friend and ally of Rome' merely disguised the fact that henceforth he was in reality reduced to that of client status. He spent the rest of his reign studiously avoiding giving cause for any further Roman intervention in Macedonian affairs, but at the same time rebuilding and rearming his military in the event that a clash might occur in the future. Perseus, Philip's son, the last Antigonid monarch of Macedonia, foolishly embroiled himself in that war with the Roman Empire. He was defeated at Pydna by L. Aemilius Paullus in 168, and paid the price for his temerity by ending his days in close confinement in an Italian villa.

The Antigonid Dynasty of Macedonia	
Antigonus Monopthalmos	d. 301
Demetrius I Poliorcetes	294–287
Antigonus II Gonnatus	279–239
Demetrius II	239–229
Antigonus III Doson	229–221
Philip V	221–179
Perseus	179–168

Macedonia was then divided into four quasi-independent states, an unsatisfactory solution but one which emphasized Roman unease at installing a presence east of the Ionian Sea. However, revolts in Greece and especially in Macedonia led by Andriscus meant that in 146, in line with momentous changes around the entire Mediterranean world, the former kingdom was transformed into a part of a new Roman *provincia* or province of Achaea.[2] The scale and rapidity of the changes affecting the Central and Western Mediterranean in this period can most easily be appreciated and its extent most vividly gauged through the table included here.

Main events in the West 264–146		
Date BC	Event	Result
264–241	The First Punic War	Rome acquired Central and Western Sicily as its first overseas possession.
238	Revolt of Carthaginian mercenaries in Sardinia & Corsica	Rome acquired Sardinia and Corsica as additional overseas territories and so created 'Mare Nostrum'.
220s	Roman intervention in the Adriatic	Client states and allies established along the coast of Illyria and Epirus.
218–201	The Second Punic War	With the defeat of Hannibal at Zama in 202, Rome obtained eastern and southern Spain, and received annual tribute from Carthage.
197	Provincial reorganisation	The new Spanish possessions were converted into two provinces: Hispania Citerior and Hispania Ulterior.
215–205	First Macedonian War	Rome foiled Macedonian attempts to relieve Hannibal in southern Italy, but the peace treaty of Phoenice was based on the status quo.
200–197	Second Macedonian War	Macedonia confined to its traditional borders and paid war indemnity to Rome.
167	Third Macedonian War	Macedonian kingdom broken up into four independent states.
149–146	Third Punic War	Carthage besieged and destroyed. The region including the major cities of Utica and Hippo became the province of Africa in 146.
146	Achaean War and Revolt of Andriscus	Corinth destroyed in 146. Greece and Macedonia merged as a single province.

The famous declaration of the Greek historian Polybius (1.1.5), that Rome had come to control nearly the whole of the known world by 167, is to be found in the preface to his history devoted to recounting that phenomenon. He relates in detail the events from Hannibal's invasion of Italy in 218 to the defeat of Perseus, but in the course of his coverage of affairs around the Mediterranean he confirms that there was no Roman permanent settlement in Asia nor does there seem to have been any intention for such in the period on which he focuses.[3] As the map clearly shows, even in 146 Rome had no overseas possessions east of the Aegean Sea (see Map 2). However, that does not mean that the Romans were unfamiliar with this region or that its many rulers were equally unacquainted with Rome. Rome's earliest ties with Greece go back to the fourth century BC, if not considerably earlier.[4] Although no Roman armies crossed the Adriatic before 229, the Romans had actually established diplomatic contacts with Ptolemaic Egypt around 273.[5] An embassy from Ptolemy II Philadelphus arrived in Rome seeking friendship and, having been favourably received by the senate, the Romans responded by sending their own ambassadors to Alexandria not long afterwards in 270/69. By then the Ptolemaic dynasty had been in control of Egypt for barely fifty years, and its incumbent ruler, following the example of his father, was astute enough to explore all possible avenues for foreign connections and support when faced with unstable borders in the Levant where warfare was almost continual.[6] The recent Roman defeat of Pyrrhus, king of Epirus, who had campaigned in southern Italy on behalf of his allies the Tarentines, must surely have attracted the attention of Ptolemy. Pyrrhus was one of the most dynamic of the kings who came after Alexander, and one who could claim a real family tie with that former monarch. A defeat at the hands of the Romans was bound to make headline news around the Hellenistic World. The high level of diplomatic contact and its evident cordiality suggests that Ptolemy had lent no aid or encouragement to Pyrrhus in his overseas adventures.[7] The contact between the two states almost certainly spurred on the Roman government to issue its first silver coinage, a sure indication of both the adoption of a full fiscal system at home, and the desire to be incorporated into the wider financial structure of the international community.[8] And while contacts after 269 may have been sporadic, they were maintained during Rome's first war with Carthage, which witnessed intensive campaigning throughout Sicily and an invasion of North Africa.

The Roman attack on Carthage, which was nearly disastrous to Rome, may well have been in deliberate emulation of a similar invasion of Africa by Agathocles, tyrant and then king of Syracuse (316–289), who campaigned right up to the walls of Carthage for several years, the only time an army led by a Greek did so. However, the debacle, the execution of Regulus, the Roman

Ptolemaic Dynasty of Egypt	
Ptolemy I Lagus	304–283/2
Ptolemy II Philadelphus	285–246
Ptolemy III Euergetes	246–221
Ptolemy IV Philopater	221–205
Ptolemy V Epiphanes	205–180
Ptolemy VI Philometor	180–145
Ptolemy VII Neos Philopater	145
Ptolemy VIII Euergetes	145–116
Ptolemy IX Soter	116–107 & 88-80
Ptolemy X Alexander	107–88
Ptolemy XI Alexander	80
Ptolemy XII Neos Dionysus	80–58
Berenice IV	58–55
Ptolemy XII	55–51 (restored)
Cleopatra VII	51–30

general, and the subsequent Roman recovery and finally Carthaginian capitulation and evacuation of Lilybaeum, its last stronghold in western Sicily, will
have been closely watched by Ptolemy II, and after his death in 246, by his son
Ptolemy III Euergetes. The change in rulers does not appear to have affected
the ties between the two states, although the new Egyptian king's interests were
mainly towards the east, with an invasion of Mesopotamia, rather than to the
west. This treaty was initially one between equals,[9] and this evidently remained
so down to about 210 when the Romans requested grain shipments from Egypt
(Livy, 27.4.10) to help them overcome shortfalls in their supplies caused by
Hannibal's presence on Italian soil.[10] But by 203 Rome was clearly in the
superior position brought on by the premature death of Ptolemy IV Philopater,
and the accession of Ptolemy V Epiphanes, who was still a child.[11] A further
Roman embassy, which was active in the eastern Mediterranean soon after the
end of hostilities with Carthage, from late 201 or early 200 returning in 199,[12]
illustrates keen and continued senatorial interest in affairs affecting the whole
of the Hellenistic World.[13] Some or all members of this legation are said to
have visited Alexandria and reinforced the earlier ties between the two states.[14]

There had also been contact with other Greek cities in the third century and
this too became a regular feature of Roman diplomacy. Apollonia in Epirus had
sent an embassy to Rome in about 266,[15] and several states on the western side
of Greece including Corcyra and Epidamnus were allies of Rome by the 220s,[16]
while the Roman invasion of Sicily in 264 could be described as nothing more
than a case of intervention in western Greek affairs. The Roman senate must
have considered that a Carthaginian occupation of Messana was a real threat to
its own security in southern Italy. However, the Carthaginians had occupied
this city before, but not at a time when the Romans had control of the Greek
cities on the mainland side of the Straits.[17] Rhegium on the mainland was
within sight of Messana, and so Rome went to war, not so much in response to
the appeal of the Campanian Mamertini, who then occupied Messana, but as a
proactive gesture aimed at protecting its Greek possessions in southern Italy.
In 241, at the end of a protracted conflict with Carthage which had lasted a
generation, Rome gained more territory which had previously been ruled by
Greeks, and an alliance with Syracuse, one of the strongest Greek city states in
the Mediterranean. In later literature, ancient writers tend to play down
contacts between the Romans and the Greeks and enhance cultural differences
rather than similarities when in reality the relationship was a long and complex
one. Livy (3.33) tells of a visit to Athens by three Roman legates as early as
450 on a mission to learn about the Athenian constitution with a view to
incorporating elements into their own laws which were then in the process of
codification. The story may not be historical and simply illustrative of a desire
to be seen to be connecting with a venerable and illustrious state and its

political institutions, or indeed it may reflect a memory of some fifth century contact. Whatever the truth of the matter it is clear that the eastern Mediterranean was not beyond the Roman horizon; and it should be remembered that Troy, the birthplace of Aeneas (direct ancestor of Romulus, founder of Rome), was situated on the Hellespont in Asia Minor.[18]

Meanwhile, further intervention in Illyria in 220/19 was, as Crawford suggests, surely designed to calm the fears of allies in western Greece who felt threatened by the piratical Demetrius of Phalarus.[19] Trade was therefore safe-guarded and Rome can once again be seen to be following a long-standing practice copied from the Greeks of Italy and Sicily: that of policing the southern Adriatic and Ionian Seas.[20] The Roman and the Hellenic worlds, never very far apart, crept ever closer and from about 200 BC they had become inextricably bound together.

Chapter 2

The Seleucids of Syria

It is indeed through Troy that further connections between Rome and the East may have come about. Suetonius, the second-century-AD biographer, in his life of the emperor Claudius (AD 41–54), relates the discovery of a letter in the imperial archives which indicated that there had been contact between Rome and the Seleucid kingdom. This is generally considered to refer to sometime in the third century, and that the monarch in question was either Seleucus II (246–226) or his son Seleucus III (226–223).

> He (Claudius) allowed the people of Ilium (Troy) perpetual exemp-
> tion from taxation on the ground that they were the founders of the
> Roman nation, and read out an ancient letter of the senate and people
> of Rome written in Greek to king Seleucus in which they promised
> their friendship and an alliance on condition that he should keep
> their relatives the people of Ilium free of tribute.
>
> (Suet., *Claud*. 25.3)[1]

Although the authenticity of this document has been doubted by modern scholars, some of whom see the letter as a part of the propaganda campaign generated in the run-up to war between Rome and the Seleucids in the 190s BC, it actually fits quite well with the chronology of Rome's early foreign relations in the third century.[2] The Romans had obviously maintained various contacts with states in the eastern Mediterranean after their initial embassy to Egypt. Plutarch, writing about the same time as Suetonius, has the following information relating to Aratus of Sicyon, who was trying to reach Egypt by sea. His first ship was unable to proceed beyond Adria in the southern Peloponnese because of adverse winds. In order to avoid arrest by Spartans occupying the town, Aratus went into hiding and for some days looked out for the possibility of continuing his journey.

> Aratus spent some days in this anxious state ... but luckily, at last, a
> Roman ship happened to beach near his place of refuge. The ship
> was on its way to Syria and Aratus was able to persuade its captain to
> land him in Caria.   (Plut., *Arat*. 12.5)

From Halicarnassus in Caria he was able to sail without further danger to Alexandria. The date of this episode probably coincides with a coup led by Aratus which saw the expulsion of the latest tyrant in Sicyon in 251/0. Roman ships plying their wares from Italy to Syria were clearly not an unusual sight even by then. Furthermore, the late-Roman historian Eutropius (3.1) records an embassy which arrived in Alexandria from Rome and gives a precise date which ties in well with the testimony of Suetonius. Eutropius says that in 241 the Romans offered military assistance to Ptolemy III in his war against Seleucus II, but that the embassy arrived too late since a peace treaty had recently been signed between the two monarchs. An embassy which made a point of visiting both of these kingdoms in the aftermath of victory over Carthage is not improbable and could have been designed as a courtesy visit to update the Egyptian and Syrian kings on the new situation in the western Mediterranean.[3] It is not altogether surprising that contact with a Seleucid king should be so close in time to the start of Romano-Egyptian relations. The Ptolemies and Seleucids were frequently in conflict yet were also very closely related, not merely ethnically but also in terms of family relations. The two families intermarried frequently throughout the tenures of their thrones.

Thus, just as the Ptolemies were relative newcomers to power in Egypt when they first had contact with Rome, so too were their closest neighbours, the rulers of a state which in the third century extended from Asia Minor in the west to the Hindu Kush in the east. This is named today the Seleucid Empire after Seleucus Nicator who, like Ptolemy Lagus, had been one of Alexander the Great's *hetairoi* or Companions. In the unstable times following the death of the Macedonian monarch in 323, he was eventually able to carve out a state which came closest to restoring Alexander's realm. As Bosworth says:

> Seleucus' rise to power is perhaps the most spectacular phenomenon
> of the period of the Successors.[4]

In the division of power following Alexander's death, Seleucus had originally obtained the governorship of Babylonia, which he lost in 316 but regained in 312. This year subsequently also became recognised as his first regnal year. He was originally an ally of Antigonus, but changed his allegiance to Lysimachus ruler in Thrace, and to Ptolemy and in a confederation finally engaged and overcame his former friend at Ipsus in 301. After the battle, Seleucus was clearly the main beneficiary of the victory, and consolidated his control of Syria and Cilicia, which gave him access to the Mediterranean and an avenue through which he was able to recruit Greeks for his army and administration. He maintained a peace with Ptolemy but increasingly found himself at odds with Lysimachus whom he attacked, defeated and killed at Corupedium in 281. From there he felt secure enough to cross the Hellespont into Thrace and

The Seleucid Dynasty of Syria			
Seleucus I Nicator	311–281	Antiochus VI Epiphanes	139–138
Antiochus I Soter	281–261	Antiochus VII Sidetes	138–129
Antiochus II Theos (b. 286)	261–246	Demetrius II	129–126
Seleucus II Callinicus (b. 266)	246–226	Antiochus VIII Grypus	126–96
Antiochus (Hierax) (b. 264)	241–226	Seleucus V	95
Seleucus III Soter (b. 243)	226–223	Demetrius III	95–88
Antiochus III Megas (b. 238)	223–187	Philip I Philadelphus	95–84/3
Seleucus IV Philopater	187–175	Antiochus X	95–83
Antiochus IV Epiphanes	175–164	Antiochus XII Dionysus	87–84
Antiochus V Eupator	164–162	Seleucus VII	83–69
Demetrius I Soter	162–150	Antiochus XIII	69–64
Alexander Balas	150–145	Philip II	65–63
Demetrius II Nicator	145–140		

extend his own rule to include Lysimachus' former kingdom. Seleucus clearly had his sights on winning back his homeland, but was unable to take Macedonia from Antigonus Gonnatus[5] before his murder by Ptolemy Ceraunus in the same year.[6] By 280, therefore, a sort of accommodation had been established between the three great Hellenistic states. The capital of Seleucus' immense realm was initially at Babylon, the city where Alexander had spent his last months, but, in emulation of Alexander, this new king of Asia also became a notable founder of cities including Seleucia-on-the-Tigris (now a part of modern Baghdad) and Antioch-on-the-Orontes in Syria. Antioch became the chief city of the kingdom and became famous in antiquity, in particular, for its opulence and its excessively luxurious living standards.

In situating his main city far to the west, Seleucus meant to openly proclaim his ambition to recover Alexander's domain in its entirety. However, this also meant that his eastern provinces were neglected, and his successors were faced with numerous problems in that immense sector. Most significantly, Bactria (regions of modern-day northern Afghanistan) broke away under its satrap Diodotus in about 250,[7] when he established an independent Hellenic kingdom, which survived north of the Hindu Kush for rather more than four generations[8] and to the south for perhaps another century or so after that.[9] More threatening was the emergence of the Parthian kingdom under Arsaces south-east of the Caspian Sea, which although at first contained, by both the Seleucids and the Bactrian Greeks, effectively cut communications between these two Greek states, and ultimately overwhelmed them both.[10]

From the start, simply on account of the Seleucid Empire's size, it lacked the geographic and administrative cohesion that its smaller but more compact Hellenistic neighbours possessed. The isolation of the Greek or Macedonian rulers and their courts from their subjected populations on account of ethnic and linguistic differences naturally never fostered a high degree of loyalty or patriotic commitment.[11] The rulers could be successful in wars, but there does not appear to have been any development of integration or an intense belonging to this huge state. It began to diminish almost as quickly as it was won. This in part was because the kingdom of the Seleucids also suffered a lack of stability caused by frequent infighting within its ruling family. It all began when Antiochus II died suddenly in 246, aged only about forty-two, shortly after his marriage to Berenice, a daughter of Ptolemy II.[12] He had divorced his previous wife Laodice, who had withdrawn to Sardis, while the position of his adult sons Seleucus and Antiochus, who had accompanied their mother, at once became insecure. In fact, Seleucus, surnamed Callinicus ('The Handsome'), was proclaimed king and won outright control after a brief spell of civil war when the Ptolemaic faction at court in Antioch was eliminated. But this was immediately followed by war with Ptolemy III (246/5) who had initially come to his sister's aid and then sought revenge for her murder. He invaded Seleucid territory from the sea, which Ptolemaic navies controlled, and was welcomed first in Seleucia, the port for Antioch, and then in Antioch itself, which had proclaimed its support for his sister while she still lived, and he secured the whole of Syria before, it is claimed, he marched into Mesopotamia. Whether he actually reached Seleucia-on-the-Tigris or Babylon is highly questionable, whatever the propaganda of the reign proclaimed, since he appears back in Alexandria within a short time. Internal Egyptian affairs had summoned him back and, in his absence, his generals lost ground to the Seleucid forces in Asia Minor beyond the Taurus Mountains where Seleucus and his family and court had sought refuge and had remained at large. Antioch was retaken and Ptolemy was forced to counter an attack on his own territory in Palestine. Although Seleucus was defeated he summoned additional troops commanded by his younger brother Antiochus, surnamed Hierax ('The Hawk'), and this move was enough to bring Ptolemy to peace negotiations which resulted in a ten-year truce between Egypt and Syria in 242/1.[13]

In order to accomplish a satisfactory peace and from his point of view a very satisfactory peace settlement with Egypt, Seleucus had needed the support and cooperation of his younger brother to whom he ceded Asia Minor as a personal fiefdom. The gesture suggests not much age difference between the two, although Antiochus is described as a fourteen-year-old by Justin in his epitome of Pompeius Trogus' history (Justin, 27.3). Since Seleucus was probably between eighteen and twenty when he succeeded as king in 246, Antiochus was probably no more than a year or two younger; and Justin's evidence should probably be regarded as an error or a vague reference to youth. By the time of the peace in 241 both brothers were in their twenties and both were clearly vigorous and ambitious. Hence the start of Seleucid familial feuding which was to rear its hydra-like head time and time again until eventually the dynasty imploded. Once the warfare with Ptolemy ended, the ambitions of the brothers inevitably clashed, with Seleucus based at Antioch, and Antiochus with his mother Laodice, his most enthusiastic supporter, at Sardis. A great battle is said to have taken place between them in about 240 near Ancyra where the younger brother was victorious mainly because he had been aided by Mithridates II, king of Pontus, who had led a highly effective cavalry force of Galatian mercenaries.[14] Badly defeated, Seleucus was forced back beyond the Taurus, but Antiochus, who could not count on his allies, was not able to take full advantage of his superior position. When, at last, he did invade Mesopotamia from the north he was defeated. And so this civil strife continued for much of the rest of the reign and, in effect, for fifteen years the Seleucid kingdom was divided into two. Seleucus spent most of his time trying to regain Asia Minor from his brother while Antiochus was never able to assert any permanent presence south of the Taurus range. In the meantime, the eastern provinces were left largely to their own devices while the line of administrative command, never strong, became appreciably weaker.

After several setbacks, Seleucus at last managed to oust Antiochus from his power base, and although he eluded capture, the runaway prince was detained in Alexandria where he had fled for succour, and from where he managed to escape to die at the hands of Galatian bandits in Thrace in 227. Seleucus, at last sole king, died the following year from a riding accident. Antiochus had married a daughter of the king of Bithynia but no male heir is attested.[15] On the other hand, Seleucus left two young sons who succeeded him in turn. Seleucus III reigned briefly and was mostly involved in warfare against Pergamum although hostilities may also have been started against Egypt. In a campaign against Attalus, the king of Pergamum, he was poisoned in 223, the victim of a conspiracy originating among his most intimate entourage. His brother Antiochus, who had been posted to Babylon to supervise the eastern satrapies, succeeded among yet more internal disorder.

In the person of Antiochus III Megas ('The Great') the fortunes of the Seleucid dynasty revived. Antiochus is one of the great military figures of ancient history and certainly ranks among the greatest of the Seleucid kings, although he was undoubtedly not even close to the other great generals of history, as we shall see.[16] He first had to contend with unrest in his eastern provinces and in order to do so was forced to allow his cousin Achaeus control over Asia Minor.

> Achaeus was a relative of that Antiochus who had just succeeded to
> the throne of Syria ... on the death of Seleucus, the father of this

Antiochus, his eldest son Seleucus had succeeded him, and Achaeus
in his capacity as a relative accompanied the king on his campaign
across the Taurus . . . The young king Seleucus . . . had learned that
Attalus (of Pergamum) had taken all his territories on this side of the
Taurus and so had hurried to defend his interests. He crossed the
Taurus with a large army but was murdered by the Gaul Apaturius
and Nicanor, Achaeus . . . at once avenged his death . . . and took
command of the army and the direction of affairs and conducted
both sensibly and with good grace. Although he was eagerly urged
on by his troops to become king and although his prospects were
favourable he refused and held the throne for the younger brother
Antiochus. He advanced confidently and recovered the country this
side of the Taurus.   (Polyb., 4.48.6–9)

And history repeated itself here: first there had been Eumenes and then Attalus
of Pergamum, and there had also been Antiochus Hierax, and now Achaeus
established himself from 222 as an independent ruler while Antiochus was
occupied with his other unruly satraps.

    . . . when he (Achaeus) was successful beyond his expectations and
    had besieged Attalus in Pergamum and was in control of the entire
    region he was so elated at his good fortune that he very quickly
    turned away from his allegiance and took to wearing the diadem and
    calling himself king and was at that moment the most formidable and
    striking of all the kings and leaders on this side of the Taurus.
                                                        (Polyb., 4.48.11–13)

This situation was to remain for some considerable time until Antiochus was
able to turn his full attention to the region, for in the meantime war with Egypt
intervened and left Achaeus at large.

Since Seleucia, Antioch's port continued to be garrisoned by a Ptolemaic
force since Ptolemy III had taken the city in 246/5, it was felt necessary to
retrieve this centre before proceeding to more ambitious plans. The city and its
harbour were surrendered to the king after a short siege and assault (Polyb.,
5.60–61).[17] Then Antiochus invaded Coele-Syria (now the Bekaa Valley in
Lebanon) and Aradus, Berytus (Beirut) and other coastal cities quickly
switched allegiance from Ptolemy to the Syrian king. Antiochus had allies in
southern Palestine, former mercenaries of Ptolemy and it was to aid these that
he plunged southwards with the bulk of his army following more sedately
behind. The Egyptian response was slow: Ptolemy IV Philopater had no reputation as a warrior, and his counsellors urged caution and diplomacy to buy

time to mobilise their forces. Antiochus, no diplomat, fell into the trap. Negotiations began and became drawn out, neither side convincing the other of its
complaints against aggressions (Egypt) or excuses for aggression (Syria).
Ptolemy at last moved his army to intercept the invader.

> Ptolemy made camp fifty stadia [roughly 10km or about 6 miles]
> from Raphia which is the first city inside Coele-Syria ... Antiochus
> approached at the same time with his army and reached Gaza, rested
> his forces and moved forward slowly. He passed Raphia and made
> camp at night about ten stadia [2km or barely more than a mile] from
> his enemy. To begin with the armies remained separated by this
> distance but after a few days, Antiochus wanting to secure a more
> favourable position for his camp and aiming to stir up the passions of
> his troops chose a spot very close to that of Ptolemy. Skirmishing
> now regularly took place between watering and foraging parties and
> there were sometimes exchanges of missiles between cavalry and
> even infantry.
>
> After they remained in their camps for some five days both kings
> decided to resolve the matter by battle. As soon as Ptolemy moved
> his army out Antiochus did likewise. Both placed phalanxes of
> picked infantry armed in the Macedonian manner in the centre
> against one another. Polycrates with his cavalry commanded the far
> left wing ... on the extreme right was Echecrates with his cavalry. Of
> the seventy-three elephants forty were placed on the centre left
> where Ptolemy was to take command and the remainder were in
> front of the centre right. Antiochus on the other hand positioned
> sixty elephants ... in front of his centre right opposite Ptolemy.
>
> When the armies were drawn up both kings rode along their lines
> with their commanders and friends and spoke to their soldiers. When
> Ptolemy and his sister Arsinoe had reached the end of his left wing
> and Antiochus, with his household guards, his right wing they
> signalled the start of the battle and instructed that the elephants were
> brought first into action.   (Pol. 5.80.1–84.1)

The two sides were finally a mere 5 stades apart (1,212 yards or 1,200 metres),
with frequent skirmishing between the opponents until Ptolemy, says Polybius
(5.81.2), made the first move for a pitched battle by moving his army out of its
camp and into a line for engagement. It is claimed that both kings made their
way along the front lines of their respective armies issuing confidence-boosting
messages until Antiochus, with his guard of cavalry, came to the end of his
right wing over which he had taken command, and Ptolemy and his sister
Arsinoe came to the end of their left wing, where the Egyptian king was

commander. At that juncture battle was joined as both kings issued orders for the start of hostilities, with their war elephants first to engage.[18] It is claimed that the African elephants of Ptolemy were uncomfortable with the Indian elephants of Antiochus and soon became disorganised and as much trouble to their own side as to their enemy.[19] Antiochus led a charge in the furthest point of the Egyptian left wing which began to fall back, while Ptolemy took refuge with his main phalanx at the centre and his own right wing got the upper hand over the Syrian left, which crumbled. Ptolemy's appearance among his own phalangites gave them heart and they advanced strongly against the Syrian centre opposite until that gave way. Antiochus had continued his pursuit of the enemy cavalry from the opposing wing instead of rounding on the enemy's centre, a cardinal error in an ancient battle which cost his army dearly. Echecrates in command of the Ptolemaic right wing had done precisely this and so sown up the victory for his own side.

> Antiochus ... being still young and inexperienced and supposing from his own success that his army was victorious in other parts of the field as well was still pursing fugitives. Finally, one his more experienced officers drew his attention to the fact that the cloud of dust was moving from the phalanx towards his own camp and he realised what had happened and attempted to return to the battlefield with his bodyguard. However, he found that the centre and left wing had retreated and so he retired to Raphia in the belief that as far as he was concerned he had done enough to win the battle but had received this defeat on account of the cowardly behaviour of others.
>
> (Polyb., 5.85.11–13)

Meanwhile Ptolemy flushed with an unexpected victory (Polyb., 5.87.3) retired to his own camp, and next day after burying his own dead, but not the bodies of the defeated, he advanced on the city of Raphia. Antiochus retired to Gaza and sent heralds requesting permission to collect and bury his dead. Polybius (5.86.5–6) gives figures for the casualties: Antiochus 10,000 infantry, 300 cavalry, 5 elephants; Ptolemy 1,500 infantry, 700 cavalry, and 16 elephants, but all his other elephants apparently taken captive. These statistics seem fair and realistic in the circumstances because the main death toll on the Syrian side occurred when its phalanx at the centre broke and turned from the Egyptian advance. The numbers involved moreover indicate a not particularly devastating defeat for Antiochus and not an entirely overwhelming victory for Ptolemy. Both retained formidable armies once they could regroup. However, it signalled the end, for the time being at least, of Antiochus' hopes of conquering the entire Levant. Coele-Syria stayed, although not very firmly, within Ptolemaic jurisdiction.[20]

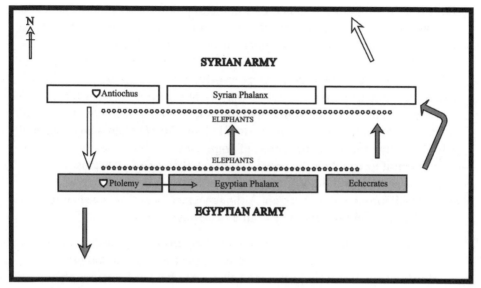

The Battle of Raphia.

The battle of Raphia, near modern Rafah in the Gaza Strip, took place on 22 June 217, and is certainly best remembered for the number of combatants in the field which, between the two sides, came close to 150,000.[21] This total probably represents the greatest number of soldiers to take the field since the engagements of Alexander the Great against Darius III at Issus in 334 and at Gaugamela in 331, and since the monumental Greek fight against the Persians at Plataea in 479. The perhaps surprising result of the battle of Raphia had left Antiochus damaged but not humbled. And within a year he set about regaining Asia Minor, with both his eastern and southern frontiers now settled.

> Antiochus made preparations on a large scale during the winter and at the beginning of the summer crossed the Taurus, and since he had reached an agreement with Attalus of Pergamum he began a joint campaign against Achaeus.[22]   (Polyb., 5.107.4)

The reason for the treaty with Attalus is not difficult to find since Achaeus posed a more immediate threat to his position in western Asia Minor than a Syrian king who had problems elsewhere. The intention of course was the classic pincer movement to catch the enemy between two invading armies. And it seems that Achaeus was driven back fairly quickly to Sardis where he was confined and besieged during the first campaigning season (Polyb., 8.15.1–18.10). Polybius again our main narrative source is fragmentary here, but it does appear as if Antiochus was soon in a dominant position. This further

illustrates the difference between the compelling power and aura of the legitimate king opposed to a pretender, however close that man might be to the royal
family. Hierax had similarly been finally overcome by Seleucus his brother the
king, and now Achaeus, after several years of what seemed to be complete
independence was brought down more swiftly than can have been anticipated.
The Syrian besiegers gained access to the city but the pro-Achaeus forces with
their king and his wife and family were still at large in the citadel.[23] His end did
not come about for at least another year if Polybius' dating here is accurate and
only then after the implementation of some clever subterfuge. Achaeus was
advised that if he could escape under cover of darkness and in disguise and then
race off to Syria he would be greeted with enthusiasm by those opposed to the
king. He fell into the prepared trap. Although a member of the royal family, his
elevated status did not save him from a gruesome end.[24]

> ... there were many proposals about the appropriate punishment to
> inflict on Achaeus, and it was decided in the first place to lop off the
> limbs of the unhappy prince, and then after his head was cut off it
> would be sown up in the skin of an ass and his body crucified. When
> this had been done and the army was informed of what had taken
> place there was such great rejoicing in the camp that Laodice who
> alone knew about her husband's departure realised the truth.[25]
>
> (Polyb., 8.21.2–4)

Shortly afterwards the citadel surrendered, and so finally by 214 Antiochus was
able to reclaim this major and extremely wealthy lost sector of his empire,
including Sardis, which was restored following the ravages it endured after the
protracted siege and subsequent sack. The campaign leading to the re-conquest
of this area brought about strange bedfellows in that Antiochus became allied
with Attalus who had himself usurped control of Asia Minor after the fall of
Hierax in 227. The alliance between these two states was to be problematic
later.[26]

Another campaign in the east drew Antiochus away between 211 and 206
with heavy fighting against Arsaces and the Parthians in Media and Hyrcania.
Polybius is again not very complimentary although Antiochus was campaigning
further east than any other Greek, with the exception of Alexander the Great
and his own grandfather and great-grandfather (Polyb., 10.27–31). The terrain
north of Ecbatana was clearly inhospitable and difficult yet Antiochus was able
to return from the region following a number of victories. Polybius is grudging
in his description of what was clearly for Antiochus a successful war., not only
against this fledgling Parthian state but also against fellow Greeks at Tapuria
on the River Arius (Polyb. 10.49.1), there in a battle against Euthydemus, king
or one of the kings of Bactria, Antiochus gained a decisive victory which caused

the Bactrian monarch to retreat into his own territory. Of course, with hindsight it is clear that fighting between the various Greeks who had settled in the
East caused them all to be weakened and easier to be taken by the Parthians.

> In this episode it appears that Antiochus fought more heroically than
> any of those around him. There were many deaths on both sides,
> but the king's cavalry threw back the first attack of the Bactrians.
> However, when a second and a third assault came the king was in
> difficulties and his men were at a loss. At that point Panaetolus
> ordered his men forward to join the king and those fighting with him
> and forced those Bactrians who were in pursuit in some disorder to
> turn their reins and retreat rapidly. In this battle Antiochus lost his
> horse which was killed by a spear and he also received a wound to his
> mouth and lost several teeth, but in general gained a greater repu-
> tation for courage on this occasion than on any other.
>
> (Polyb., 10.49.9–14)

The death of Ptolemy IV in 205/4 and the accession of the child Ptolemy V
Epiphanes about a year later obviously wetted Antiochus' appetite for further
possible expansion on his southern boundaries; and, as he would no doubt have
seen it, as correcting the situation which had been the result of Raphia in 217.[27]

Antiochus was again the aggressor but we have far less detail on this
campaign since Polybius' history survives only in fragments, and other later
historians such as Livy were not interested in events if they did not affect the
Romans directly. This new invasion of Coele-Syria in 200 by Antiochus
culminated in the Battle of Panion, the outcome of which was directly related
to the later war of Antiochus in Greece and Asia Minor against Rome since it
gave him a settled southern frontier, and allowed him freedom of action in Asia
Minor. Moreover, it was a boost to his ego some would say leading to over-
confidence, to take on the Romans. Polybius probably covered this episode
in detail, unluckily the material which survives is a hostile criticism of his
source, a historian named Zeno, whose account he found seriously at fault, not
he says of deliberate inaccuracy but from an over-zealous attachment to style
which saw him sacrifice the truth for textual beauty. Therefore, an unreliable
historian is the source of a narrative which is itself a fragment. Polybius
(16.18.1–19.11) is more concerned about showing the inadequacy of Zeno's
incoherent account rather than providing a better narrative himself. Of course,
that may well have existed in the extant history which has been lost. Zeno gives
information which is clearly impossible to believe: that Antiochus had two sons
both named Antiochus with him on this campaign that when the opposing
phalangites engaged the war elephants fought amid the close encounter of
the heavy infantry.[28] Antiochus probably commanded the cavalry on the right

wing as he usually did, and on this occasion, after nearly two decades of battle experience, managed to wheel his horsemen victorious on that side to attack the Ptolemaic phalanx from the rear. Scopas the Egyptian commander evidently retreated when the issue became obvious. Some measure of Polybius' derision at the account he had in front of him can be gauged.

> Writers it seems to me should be thoroughly ashamed of such non-sensical errors. They should strive to become masters of the whole art of writing history, for that is the best course. If this is beyond their intellect then they should at least give the closest attention to what is absolutely necessary and important.
>
> (Polyb., 16.20.1–2)

Coele-Syria became a Seleucid province, and the young king Ptolemy V was married to Antiochus' daughter Cleopatra. It was the Syrian king's greatest moment. Not only that but the victory at Panion was a significant point in his career and emboldened his attitude to other powers, particularly Rome, which had just at that point emerged triumphant from its long conflict with Carthage. It was also precisely at the point where relations between Rome and Philip V of Macedonia had reached new lows to the extent that war had been declared by the Roman senate. Antiochus flushed from his successes could view these new hostilities with some comfort and considerable interest from Antioch.

Chapter 3

The States of Asia Minor

It is considerably more than a thousand kilometres from the city of Istanbul in Turkey to Tbilisi, the capital of modern Georgia, and roughly the same from the Dardanelles (the ancient Hellespont) to Lake Van in Armenia, a distance which transcribes a region that in antiquity was called Asia Minor. More precisely, in antiquity this comprised all the lands inland from the Hellespont and the Aegean Sea to the west, flanked by the Euxine or Black Sea to the north and the eastern Mediterranean to the south, and across the Anatolian uplands as far as the River Halys and the Taurus Mountains, which marked its frontier from the greater landmass which was known even then as Greater Asia, the continent. From the first century AD the region regularly appears as Asia Minor in literary texts.[1] Asia Minor comprised numerous subdivisions: along the coastal plains, Pontus, Paphlagonia, Bithynia, Troad, Mysia, Aeolia, Ionia, Lydia, Caria, Lycia, Pisidia, Pamphylia, and Cilicia; inland Phrygia, Galatia, Cappadocia and Lycaonia (see Map 5). Much of this territory was administered by satraps of the Persian Empire, from the sixth century down to their conquest by Alexander the Great between 334 and 332, comprising the satrapies of Cilicia, Lydia and Hellespontine Phrygia or Dascylium. Alexander's celebrated exploit of cutting the 'knot' at Gordium, the chief city of Phrygia, obscure the fact that in his hurry to engage his army with that of the Persian king Darius III, it was the furthest inland he travelled in Asia Minor before heading south-east towards the Cilician Gates and the heartland of the Persian Empire. The peoples of the interior were relatively untouched by the Macedonian invasion and rulers, whether Greek or Persian appointments, were left under the super-vision of Macedonians generals such as Antigonus Monophthalmos ('The One-Eyed'), made satrap of Hellespontine Phrygia as Alexander passed by.

Much of the urban culture in this region was Hellenic or heavily influenced by the Greeks. Indeed, at the western end, Ionia was the birthplace of many notable literary figures, artists and philosophers: Hecataeus, the earliest chronicler came from Ionian Miletus, while Halicarnassus in Caria could boast Herodotus, the first historian, as its son. In the wars which followed the death of Alexander, Asia Minor as a whole initially remained under the control of Antigonus and his son Demetrius Poliorcetes ('The Besieger'), but following the battle of Ipsus in 301, where the former was killed and the latter had fled to

Greece, it was added to the domain of Seleucus I Nicator. Yet, very soon many of these regions broke away from any centralized control to form independent states, often governed by kings. The most significant for this study are discussed here. The situation under the first Seleucus did remain a permanent one and even within the reign of the fourth Seleucid, the uprising of Antiochus Hierax did much damage to Syrian power here and allowed others to gain ultimately from this civil war. To regain this entire region for his empire, after stabilizing his eastern provinces, became a driving ambition of Antiochus III.

Bithynia

According to Appian (*Mith.* 1.1–2) the first ruler of Bithynia was Bithys, a son of Zeus and Thrace, and that after him forty-nine kings ruled in succession down to the second century BC. About 220 BC Prusias I, king of Bithynia between about 230 and 182, was at war with Byzantium (Polyb. 4.48.13–49.3), on a seemingly trivial issue of locally voted statues to the monarch which had failed to materialise.

> One of Prusias' grievances against the Byzantines was that after they had voted to erect certain statues of him they had not done so and appeared to have neglected and forgotten the affair.
>
> (Polyb. 4.49.1)

More relevant was probably an attempt by the Byzantines to marginalize the Bithynian king by promoting a peace between Achaeus, independent ruler in Asia Minor at the start of the reign of Antiochus III, and Attalus of Pergamum. However, Prusias may also have had his eye on the strategically important and well-fortified site on the western side of the Propontis, and so an expansion in his own power as a result of an important acquisition or by subordinating the Byzantines to his will. He was certainly capable enough of maintaining his place in the region, having annihilated Gallic tribesmen who in 218 were causing havoc in the Hellespont.

> Prusias ... led an army against the Gauls and after he destroyed the men in a battle he killed nearly all the women and children and allowed his soldiers to plunder the Gallic baggage train. By this victory he freed the Hellespontine cities from a serious threat and danger, and he gave as a good lesson a warning to the European barbarians not in future to be quick to cross over into Asia.
>
> (Polyb., 5.111.6–8)

His son and successor Prusias II (182–149) was a brother-in-law of Perseus, last king of Macedonia, and remained neutral in the Third Macedonian War (170–168), but escaped punitive action by the Romans for this unwise move after their defeat of the Macedonians. His relations with Attalus II, king of Pergamum, were stormy and a full-scale war broke out in 156 when Prusias ignored Roman orders for negotiations and launched an attack which resulted in a siege of Pergamum.[2] A second legation from Rome ordering a cessation to hostilities was however obeyed and Prusias was obliged to pay his neighbour compensation to the tune of 500 talents and twenty warships (App., *Mith.* 17–3).[3] Prusias II was not a popular king with his subjects who looked forward to a time when his son Nicomedes would become king. Nicomedes who had already been seen as a threat had been sent to live in Rome by the king. A certain Menas, an ambassador from Prusias to the senate, formed a conspiracy with Nicomedes against the king and persuaded Andronicus, an ambassador of Attalus, to seek the king of Pergamum's active support in expelling Prusias and replacing him with his son. Attalus did indeed throw his support behind the young man and with Pergamene troops supplementing a small force of Bithynian supporters Nicomedes led an invasion of his father's kingdom. Prusias expected Roman support and retired to his stronghold at Nicaea. The Roman senate delayed sending an embassy, but when this finally arrived in Bithynia and ordered the hostilities to cease, while Nicomedes and his backer Attalus appeared to comply, they suggested that there were sufficient complaints against the king to warrant further investigation by the senate.[4] The envoys agreed and left matters incomplete returning to Rome for further guidance. In the meantime Prusias lost heart that support would be forthcoming and retreated to Nicomedia where the citizens opened the gates to Nicomedes. Prusias fled to the temple of Zeus where he was murdered by one of Nicomedes' supporters. Nicomedes succeeded to the throne.[5]

Cappadocia

Appian is rather confused about the early history of Cappadocia and its people (*Mith.* 2.8). Clearly his source was deficient here in comparison with Bithynia. The entire region of Asia Minor had been under Persian control from the time of Cyrus the Great's (550–530) conquest of the Lydian kingdom of Croesus in 547/6. When Alexander invaded in 334 the Persian satraps of Asia Minor had fought against the Macedonians and lost. Some quickly came to terms and were left in place. When Alexander returned from his great expedition into the heart of Asia as far as the Indus valley he found that many of the officials he had appointed had indulged in corrupt practices and were executed or relieved of their duties. Ariarathes, ruler of Cappadocia, was hanged by Perdiccas, either says Appian because he had rebelled or because the Macedonian regent felt it was time to impose direct rule. Eumenes of Cardia, who had been in charge of Alexander's finances, was appointed governor, but following his execution by Antigonus after the Battle of Gabiene in 316, the Antigonids took full control.

Antigonus appointed a Greek named Nicanor as ruler and later ruled the province himself. Appian says (*Mith.* 2.9) that there was a certain Mithridates among Antigonus' company, who was related to the family of Darius, the last Persian king. Antigonus entertained suspicions about this man's loyalty and ordered his arrest. Mithridates escaped and set himself up in a fortress in Cappadocia and on account of the strife between the Macedonian generals at this time was left alone to exploit his good luck. He soon acquired not only the whole of Cappadocia but also other places along the Black Sea coast including Pontus. This Mithridates was the first of his line, and the Mithridates who as king fought against the Romans the sixth and the last of his dynasty. In 92 Mithridates VI was ordered by the Romans to restore Cappadocia to Ariobarzanes, then its king. If as Appian claims Cappadocia and Pontus were ruled by the same family then the former had at some stage been lost. Friction over who should rule Cappadocia was plainly one of the causes for the first of the 'Mithridatic Wars'. Mithridates initially complied with the Roman request but in 90 just before his invasion of the Roman province of Asia he caused further instability by supporting Socrates, a brother of Nicomedes of Bithynia, in an unlawful occupation and intrigued in Cappadocian affairs so that Ariobazanes was driven out and replaced by Ariarathes (*Mith.* 2.10).

Pergamum

Considering its imposing situation high above the coastal plain of northern Ionia, it is surprising that Pergamum had no ancient history, but emerges in the literary sources as a fortified site only towards the end of the fourth century. Philetairos is named as the commander of a garrison employed here by Lysimachus, one of Alexander's successors, who had made himself king of Thrace. Philetairos switched his allegiance from Lysimachus to Seleucus, king of Syria, shortly after the battle of Ipsus in 301. And after the murder of Seleucus, a power vacuum in Asia Minor allowed this general the freedom to enlarge his own power base and create an independent state. His successor Eumenes, a nephew, maintained his independent status and may have begun calling himself king of Pergamum before his death in 241.[6] His son Attalus I (241–197) was certainly recognised as a monarch throughout the region and did particularly well out of the conflict in the Syrian royal house after 241, and even more so from his friendship with Rome whose side he loyally followed in the war against Philip V of Macedonia. Indeed his successor Eumenes II (197–159) was able to absorb much of what in the opinion of the rulers at Antioch was the most westerly of its possessions after the battle of Magnesia-ad-Sipylum in 189. Pergamum's resolute and mostly successful defence of Hellenism in western Asia Minor from attacks such as those by Gallic tribes resulted in a web of diplomatic ties with the numerous Greek cities in the region, which willingly placed themselves under this state's influence. Pergamum's room for expansion was inevitably constrained after the Roman presence in Asia became permanent, but it also retained strong and mostly friendly links with Rome in the fifty years after the defeat of Syria.

In 133 Pergamum was bequeathed to the Roman people by the will of its last king Attalus III who had no close heirs. The kingdom was, however, immediately plunged into chaos by this action because of a rebellion against the Roman takeover led by an individual named Aristonicus. This man was possibly related to the former dynasty, but whatever his origins he was popular and attracted much support and fought successfully against Roman armies for about three years. During this time Aristonicus proclaimed himself Eumenes III and issued coins bearing this title in order to pay his troops. He was eventually captured and executed though only after inflicting some embarrassing defeats on the Romans. After the rebellion was squashed a commission of ten senators was despatched to supervise the incorporation of the state as a Roman province. The *senatus consultum de agro Pergameno*, which has survived on stone and which deals with the collection of tribute from the new province, is probably to be dated within a generation of its settlement. The new province was named Asia, but the seat of the governor was moved at some stage to Ephesus.[7] The city and the province initially saw few benefits from Roman rule. Embroiled in the Mithridatic Wars and then the civil wars which caused the end of senatorial government at Rome, the province was actually pauperised. However, with the advent of a universal peace under the autocrat Augustus, prosperity returned to the region and cities such as Pergamum and Ephesus flourished for hundreds of years under stable Roman rule.

Rhodes

Rhodes had been a major power in Greek affairs ever since the cities on the island unified to form a single *polis* in 408/7 BC. This synoicism enabled the united island to extend its influence in military affairs and acquire territory overseas, either in the Aegean or on mainland Asia Minor. Its power ultimately rested on its formidable fleets and the wealth it derived from trade, and it made and broke treaties to suit its ambitions, as war with Byzantium in alliance with Prusias (Polybius 4.48.13) king of Bithynia illustrates. At other times an ally of the Ptolemies who were sufficiently far removed from the region, it viewed any expansionist tendencies by Syria or Macedonia on the other hand as a direct threat to its independence; and, indeed, it was one of those states along with Pergamum and Athens which sought early ties with Rome. Initially doing well from its alliance with the Romans and repaid liberally for its aid in naval power which it lent to the Rome against Antiochus III, Rhodes eventually fell from favour. A positive description of the Rhodians by Polybius (5.88–91) is possibly influenced by events during his own career down to 168. However, Rhodes was never the same after the defeat of Perseus at the battle of Pydna, for Roman perceptions that the Rhodians had been meddling in affairs which did not concern them caused an atmosphere of distrust to grow between them. The Rhodians had pressed for a modus vivendi between Macedonia and Rome, which was not at all to the liking of the latter which suspected a pro-Perseus stance among the Rhodian leadership. The creation of the island of Delos as a free port under Athenian supervision soon after the defeat of Macedonia crippled Rhodes and ruined its former prosperity and influence in the eastern Mediterranean.

Armenia

Armenia was a satrapy of the Persian Empire from the time it was taken by Cyrus soon after 550 down to its conquest by Alexander. After Alexander's death it had been a part of the realm of Antigonus and seems to have been administered by the same Mithridates who later set himself up as ruler of Cappadocia. After Ipsus it reverted to rule by the Seleucids, but these appear to have had no more than a tenuous grip over this large and mountainous region. After the defeat of Antiochus III at Magnesia-ad-Sipylum in 189 Armenia achieved an independent status under a king named as Artaxias. Its most famous monarch was Tigranes I 'the Great' (*c*.100–56) who extended his territory south and east at the expense of both the Parthian and the Seleucid kingdoms. Indeed Tigranes occupied much of Syria by 70 and effectively brought an end to the Seleucid dynasty. In 69 his alliance with Mithridates of Pontus brought disaster and defeat at the hands of Lucullus who captured his newly built capital at Tigranocerta and, as a result, he sought terms from Pompey in 66 who allowed him to retain the kingship of Armenia but with the loss of all other recent conquests. Thereafter Armenia remained a buffer between Rome and the kingdom of Parthia. Sometimes formally a client state of Rome its kings were also often highly influenced by the Parthians who regarded the region as their own. The severity of the winter weather in Armenia is dramatically described by Xenophon in his *Anabasis*:

> Next there was a three days' march of forty-five miles over level ground through deep snow. On the third day's march the going was hard because of a north wind which blew into their faces and cut everything in its path like a knife and froze people stiff.
>
> (*Anab.* 4.5)

Chapter 4

Rome and Antiochus III

By the end of the Second Punic War Rome was not only suspicious of the possible expansionist policies of Philip V of Macedonia, but also of the aspirations of the Syrian king. This state of affairs, says Livy (31.14.5), arose because of a purported treaty between Philip and Antiochus dated sometime between 204 and 200 in which the two monarchs:[1]

> ... agreed to divide between them the wealth of Egypt for both of them had been looking with some longing on those riches ever since the news of Ptolemy's (IV) death had been reported.

The Ptolemaic possessions in Asia Minor and on the various eastern Mediterranean islands were certainly worth coveting, but Egypt itself was probably beyond the grasp of either Philip or Antiochus as long as a Ptolemy was available as ruler. Rome nonetheless might well have viewed such posturing with alarm especially given the established relationship between it and Egypt. However, one should note that Appian does not mention any such treaty at the start of his *Syrian Wars*, and puts the war down to the uncontrolled ambitions of Antiochus.

> He was elated by his successes and by the title which he had gained from these, he invaded Coele-Syria and a part of Cilicia, and annexed them from Ptolemy ... who was still a boy. And now consumed with unbounded ambition he campaigned against the Hellespontine, Aeolian and Ionian Greeks ... Then he crossed over to Europe and brought Thrace under his rule ... This was the start of an open disagreement with the Romans ...
>
> (App., *Syr.* 1.1–2)

Therefore, it may be the case that Livy has inserted an item which is unhistorical or at least based on hearsay from that time and used, among other things, as a pretext by the Romans in justifying the subsequent hostilities. The fact that Antiochus became Ptolemy's father-in-law in 195 does seem to cast some uncertainty about Livy's evidence suggesting the existence of ancient propaganda directed against Syria. The start of the war between Rome and the

Seleucid king is treated in some detail by Polybius, writing about fifty years after its end, who says it began on account of:

> ... the grievances harboured by the Aetolians, and how in consequence of these they summoned the help of Antiochus from Asia and so ignited the war from Asia against the Achaeans and the Romans. After I have explained the causes of this war and the way in which Antiochus crossed to Europe I shall recount firstly how he was expelled from Greece, and secondly how following his defeat in this campaign he gave up all his territories in Asia up to the Taurus Mountains, and thirdly how the Romans after crushing the warlike Gallic tribes in Galatia established undisputed control over the whole of Asia Minor and delivered its peoples west of the Taurus from the fear of barbarian invasions and the lawless activities of the Gauls.
>
> (Polyb., 3.3)

He goes on to elaborate that:

> ... it is clear that the cause of the war between Antiochus and the Romans was the anger felt by the Aetolians, who believed that they had been insulted by the Romans in a number of ways relating to the conclusion of hostilities with Philip, and so not only did they invite Antiochus to come to Greece, but they were ready to do and to suffer anything because of their resentment at certain contemporary events. The pretext for war was the so-called liberation of Greece, which the Aetolians proclaimed although it was unreasonable and untrue, as they went around each city with Antiochus. Finally the start of war was Antiochus' seizure of Demetrias.   (Polyb., 3.7)

Polybius' history of the start of this war is naturally inserted into his continuing coverage of the Roman war against Carthage which had begun in 218 and concluded after the victory of Scipio Africanus over Hannibal at Zama in 201. No sooner had this monumental struggle ended than Rome immersed itself in further warfare now with Macedonia over which the Romans triumphed at Cynoscephalae in 197. All the time diplomatic relations with Syria were ongoing as they were with Egypt but unlike with the Ptolemaic dynasty a cordial nature if once prevalent becomes less discernible. This it is not difficult to understand seeing that Antiochus, fulfilling his ambitions to measure his conquests against his ancestor Nicator, had by 196 (App., *Syr.* 1.1) established himself in Thrace and had re-founded, fortified and garrisoned Lysimacheia-on-Propontis.

By 195/4 the Roman senate having enforced a treaty on the defeated Macedonian king Philip V had probably reached the decision that Greece could be controlled at a distance. However, there were obvious reservations about a complete withdrawal of troops from this region, not least in the person of the Syrian king. Polybius again notes the disquiet:

> Decisions had already been reached in Rome on all other issues and the members of the commission had instructions on these from the senate, but because of misgivings about the intentions of Antiochus, the question of the status of Chalcis, Corinth and Demetrias had been left to their discretion taking account of the situation on the spot. It was well known that Antiochus for some time had been watching for an opportunity to intervene in Greek affairs.
>
> (Polyb., 18.45)

In the opinion of Livy, whose history of Roman foreign affairs heavily relied on Polybius' account, gives as a background to the conflict Antiochus' apparently somewhat disingenuous argument, which even then would not have stood up to rigorous scrutiny.

> He (Antiochus) had not ... sought any spoils arising from Philip's misfortunes; nor had he crossed into Europe to challenge the Romans. But he regarded as belonging to his kingdom all the lands which had once been the realm of Lysimachus, for after his defeat all the latter's possessions had passed by due right of conquest to Seleucus. He had merely come to recover his ancient right to those possessions and to refound Lysimacheia after its destruction by Thracian tribes so that Seleucus his son could have it as the capital of his kingdom.
>
> (Livy, 33.40.5–6)

The Romans might well have considered this case lacking in all merit since Seleucus had held this part of Thrace for a matter of weeks in 281 between the Battle at Corupedium and his own murder. Thrace was subsequently and very quickly given up by Seleucus' successor and the land up till then never reclaimed. It was if nothing else a piece of sophism, and one which the Roman delegation might easily dismiss. Antiochus knew he had feeble grounds in an area increasingly under review by Rome. The complaints of Lampsacus and Smyrna, among other cities in Ionia and Aeolia, were also of concern to the Romans since these had been freed from Philip's control and had simply then been absorbed into the Syrian empire. The Romans required that these be freed again. Antiochus simply did not see these complaints as sufficient a cause for war between two major powers. Indeed, some measure of the mentality of the king and his powers of concentration can be gauged by his reaction to a rumour which circulated at this point that Ptolemy V had died. He immediately broke off talks with the Roman envoys and, in the hope that he might be able to take Egypt while there was an interregnum, he set off with his entire fleet heading along the coast to Alexandria. At Patara (Livy, 33.41.5) in Pamphylia he had news that Ptolemy's death had been greatly exaggerated and so changed his plans for an attack on Cyprus, then held by Ptolemaic garrisons. Then a mutiny delayed him and no sooner was that problem solved than a violent storm caused such tremendous damage to his fleet that with winter approaching he limped home to Antioch.

> Antiochus collected what was left of his fleet after the shipwreck, and as he was now in no position to attempt anything in Cyprus he returned to Seleucia with arms far less splendid than those with which he set out. There he ordered the ships to be drawn up on land and, since winter was now approaching, he withdrew to Antioch and winter quarters.   (Livy 33.41.9–10)

Taking into account that Livy's history is liable to be extremely patriotic and therefore bias can be expected in proportion to the calibre of the enemy, Antiochus does not emerge here at least as a great or clever tactician or diplomat. Instead, like other members of his family he appears headstrong, temperamental and, at the very least, ill advised. However, Appian records that following this fiasco Antiochus celebrated the marriage of his son Antiochus to Laodice (App., *Syr.* 1.4). Athenaeus relates some information about the king's character which he obtained from Polybius. It is highly unflattering, but again illustrates the personal side of this monarch.

> When Antiochus called 'the Great', who was defeated by the Romans, arrived in Chalcis, as Polybius says in Book 20 of his history, and celebrated a wedding. He was fifty years old and was in the process of undertaking two very serious tasks, the first being the liberation of Greece the second a war with the Romans. He fell in love with a young girl from Chalcis when war had begun and was very eager to be married to her, being a lover of wine and something of a drunk. So he celebrated his wedding at Chalcis and spent the whole winter there not giving another moment's thought about the military situation. He gave the girl the name Euboea and after he was defeated in the war he fled to Ephesus with his new bride.
> (Athenaeus, 10.439 e.f.)

The intervention of Hannibal may in fact have swung the balance in favour of war, although again the biased nature of the surviving sources – if indeed there were any which put a positive bent on the Syrian side – means that the account should be handled with some caution. Hannibal was probably the most hated man in the Roman world and who certainly became a target for any subterfuge the origins of which lay at Rome. He remained powerful at Carthage for a short while after the war ended but his and his family's position (the Barcids) of supremacy came under threat. His fall was inevitable and to avoid imprisonment and death in his home city, or worse being handed over to the Romans for punishment, he fled.

> Hannibal arrived in Tyre after a good journey, and was received by these founders of Carthage as a distinguished guest from their other homeland, a man who had already covered himself in all honours. After a stay of a few days he sailed to Antioch where he was informed that the king had already departed for Asia, but he met the king's son, who was celebrating the annual games at Daphne and was welcomed warmly. Again he set sail and caught up with the king at Ephesus whom he found still equivocal in his attitude to war with Rome. However, the arrival of Hannibal had a powerful effect bringing about a final decision. The Aetolians' sentiment was also turning away from an alliance with Rome, since they had sent a legation to Rome to request the restoration of Pharsalus and Leucas, and some other cities, according to their original treaty, but the senate had referred their ambassadors to T. Quinctius.   (Livy, 33.49.5–8)

Antiochus was urged on in his ambitions by Thoas, the leader of an embassy of the Aetolian League, who promised to place all Aetolian forces at his disposal and that both Sparta and Macedonia might be sympathetic to his intervention

Main Events from 223–193	
223	Accession of Antiochus III
222/13	Rebellion of Achaeus in Asia Minor
221/20	Death of Ptolemy III
219–17	Fourth Syrian War
217	Battle of Raphia
216	Antiochus began the campaign against Achaeus
213	Sardis taken by Antiochus
211–03	Antiochus in the east
204/3	Death of Ptolemy IV
203	Accession of Ptolemy V
203	Start of the Fifth Syrian War
200	Battle of Panion
196	Antiochus re-founded Lysimacheia
195	Antiochus' abortive attack on Cyprus
195/4	Hannibal in Tyre, Antioch and Ephesus
192	Antiochus took Demetrias on Euboea
191	Battle of Thermopylae
190	Battle of Magnesia-ad-Sipylum

in Greece. The king was taken in by these words (App., *Syr*. 3.12) and, instead of waiting for his full armament which was still south of the Taurus to assemble, he decided to launch an expedition with only the troops available to him in western Asia Minor, numbering 10,000 infantry and 300 cavalry.[2] The undertaking was on a far more serious scale yet the preparations are highly reminiscent of his dash for Egypt in 195. The king's impulsive nature should clearly have been of some concern when the potential for large-scale military operations seemed imminent. The Syrian king and the Roman ambassadors had not been able to reach any agreement at their last meeting and the latter's commitment to ensuring the freedom of Greece from outside interference, in other words not their own, was liable to incur a drastic response. Yet Antiochus, although he should have been completely aware of Rome's dealings with Carthage – he had Hannibal in his court – and had seen the rapid defeat of Philip V not long beforehand still chose to ignore the possibility and believe he could win the whole of Greece with a small force. Appian says (*Syr*. 3.14) that Hannibal advised the king not to rely heavily on the Aetolians or others who claimed to be allies but rather to use half his fleet to attack the Italian coastline so that Romans would be kept busy there, try for an alliance with Philip V but failing that send an army against him to also keep him engaged elsewhere. This would leave Greece open to invasion.

> Such was the advice of Hannibal and this was the best that was offered but on account of jealousy of his reputation and judgement the other members of the king's council and the king himself ignored it entirely in case the glory of the expedition should be his ...
>
> (App., *Syr*. 3.14)[3]

The Aetolian League moved to occupy harbours on the Aegean to allow Antiochus' army friendly space to land. Demetrias (modern Volos) was particularly favoured as a stronghold worth occupying and this city renounced its alliance with Rome. So Antiochus was able to make his headquarters here for the forthcoming campaign once he crossed from Ephesus. The Romans were however also present in Boeotia where a small force of about 500 had been sent by Flamininus, who was still in the Peloponnese, to bolster the defences of Chalcis against the king. These were however overwhelmed at Delium by a Syrian force led says Appian (*Mith*. 3.12) by a general named Micithio. Livy tells the story rather differently stating that Micithio was a Chalcidian envoy and pro-Roman who had persuaded Flamininus to send the Roman force while he names the Syrian general as Menippus (Livy, 35.50). The accuracy of the writers is perhaps of less importance here than the result which saw the Chalcidians open their gates to Antiochus and the whole of Euboea falling to the invasion force within a matter of days. When they heard of Antiochus' invasion and of his success at Delium and Chalcis, the Roman response was predictable; and an army raised jointly from Roman citizens and Italian allies was despatched to cross the Adriatic by the spring of 191. And so after a decade of unease between the two powers a war between two giants finally began.

> The Romans and Antiochus had been suspicious of each other for a long time, the former believing that the king would not remain inactive because he was so puffed up by the extent of his empire and the height of fortune he had achieved. On the other hand, the king considered the Romans to be the only ones who could prevent his increase in power and his crossing into Europe.
>
> (App., *Syr.* 1.2)

Antiochus could feel quite secure on his southern frontier since he had become father-in-law to Ptolemy in 193 (App., *Syr.* 1.5), while the eastern sector of his empire must have been sufficiently quiet for him to call upon his full army, which was being brought from Syria under the command of Polyxenidas (App., *Syr.* 3.14).[4] However, the size of his army indicates again the impulsive nature of this king in that he believed that such a major undertaking could be accomplished with such a small investment. It also illustrates his naivety even after thirty years in power to have faith in allies like the Aetolians who already had a very unreliable record.[5] Nonetheless, with Euboea now his base he marched from there into Thessaly and laid siege to Larissa, one of its most powerful cities. To judge from his previous campaigns Antiochus always had a siege capability on hand: engineers and other siege specialists such as tunnellers and their various machines. Such a capability had become de rigeur since the victorious campaigns of Alexander the Great in the 330s.[6]

Although there was no love lost between the Macedonian and Seleucid dynasties, it is perhaps surprising that Philip V rather than throwing off his allegiance to Rome actually reiterated his loyalty.[7] Philip had been as headstrong as Antiochus in his younger years but seems to have acquired a more mature outlook, especially following his defeat in 197. He almost certainly realised that Antiochus stood little chance of success against Roman power and would gain more by standing aside in this war even offering help to Rome. Indeed, Appian says that a Roman army was already stationed in or near Macedonia under the command of the praetor Baebius, who, once he had the declared support of Philip, was able to despatch a detachment of 2,000 men, probably cavalry, under the command of Appius Claudius Pulcher to relieve Larissa.[8] When Claudius appeared near Larissa, Antiochus is supposed to have retreated in some disorder, giving as the excuse that it was nearly winter, but in fact afraid that the combined forces of Baebius and Philip had arrived in Thessaly. Thus his retreat from Larissa was the product of a lack of good intelligence and surveillance of his enemy's movements and, as we have seen before, a spur of the moment judgement, which hardly indicates good command, at least in the eyes of the Roman sources. Competent generals even in the Ancient World kept scouts and lookouts well-posted to indicate any sudden advance by enemy troops. Antiochus III simply was not in the class of an Alexander, a Gaius Marius or a Julius Caesar.

As already noted above, in the winter Antiochus married again and it is claimed that he spent his time in idle pursuits with his new bride, and allowed his troops to spend their time in similar inactivity. This would have been a strange behaviour for any commander having just suffered a reverse and one who surely realised that with the spring would come some serious and difficult fighting. His allies in Europe had become far less substantial with the decision of Philip to maintain his treaty with Rome. His troops too had just pulled back from a siege which they ought to have carried with ease, and their morale would have been lower as a result. We are of course reliant on pro-Roman sources so cannot verify their statements about Antiochus' erratic behaviour but, given his past behaviour, it would not have been entirely out of character. Yet at the beginning of spring Antiochus was reportedly back in the field, regretting his recent inactivity and intent on the annexing of Acarnania in western Greece. In the meantime, the newly levied Roman army was transported from Brundisium to Apollonia, numbering says Appian (*Syr.* 4.17) 20,000 infantry, 2,000 cavalry and 'a few elephants'. This army was already more than double the number available to Antiochus, and to this total could also be added the forces already in the neighbourhood of Macedonia and any proffered by Philip. Manius Acilius Glabrio, one of the consuls of 191, was in command and quickly occupied Thessaly and expelled any garrisons left by Antiochus and, with aid from Philip, subjugated Athamania, one of Antiochus' few allied states forcing its king Amynander to flee, capturing about 3,000 of Antiochus' troops.[9] The rapidity of the Roman counter-offensive so alarmed the Syrian king that he immediately sent off messengers requesting the urgent arrival of his main army but at the same time gave up any attempt of further campaigning in Acarnania. He retreated to the pass at Thermopylae in the hope that he could hold this position thus safeguarding his base on Euboea and to wait until he received reinforcements.

> The pass at Thermopylae is long and narrow and on the one side flanked by the sea which is rough and without a beach and by a steep and impassable cliff on the other side. It is overhung by two high peaks one called Teichius and the other Callidromos. The place also has hot springs hence the name 'The Hot Gates.'
>
> (App., *Syr.* 4.17)

However, it was also notorious as the place where the Persians led by Xerxes overcame a combined Hellenic army led by the Spartan king Leonidas in 480. Leonidas then had been outflanked by a Persian brigade which had used a path over the mountains scattering a detachment left there as guard and then attacking the Greeks from the rear. The majority of the Greek army was ordered to fall back by the Spartan king who then proceeded to hold the pass from combined frontal and rear attacks for just long enough for the escape to take place. Leonidas and his 300 Spartiates with about 3,000 other troops from Sparta and Thespiae were wiped out. A Theban contingent deserted to the Persians and its soldiers branded and enslaved on the order of Xerxes for cowardice. The point is that once done then the outflanking attack could easily be attempted again. Why Antiochus chose this spot and thought it favourable to his chances is mystifying as events proved.

The time has come to say something about one the most famous figures of this period of the Roman Republic, the elder Cato. Marcus Porcius Cato born about 235 was consul in 195, a *novus homo* or a 'new man', a newcomer to the highest levels of Roman politics, whose family had never before participated in public life. Although by then a senior political figure he had volunteered to enlist in the army as a military tribune, or junior officer. And in this capacity he served under the consul Glabrio whose brief was to turf Antiochus out of Greece.

Plutarch (*Cato the Elder*, 13) in his life of Cato has this to say about his subject's participation in the battle.

> Now Antiochus had blocked the narrow pass of Thermopylae with his army and strengthened the natural defences of the position by means of walls and trenches, and he remained there in confidence believing it impossible to attack him in Greece.[10] In fact, the Romans gave up hope of forcing the pass by a direct assault. Cato, however, remembered the famous outflanking manoeuvre in which the Persians had turned the defences of Leonidas and so took a large force setting out under cover of darkness.

After some hair-raising adventures as the soldiers stumbled around the rocks and chasms on a moonless night they found their objective and put to flight the 2,000 troops from the Aetolian League placed here by Antiochus to guard the infamous path (App., *Syr.* 4.18).[11] These fled to rejoin the main force in the pass but their arrival unnerved the rest who rapidly gave way to the main Roman assault. Antiochus was, as usual, in the forefront of the fighting on horseback and was hit in the mouth by a stone which shattered his teeth. His troops now subject to attack from front and rear started a mad scramble to retreat to safety. Plutarch says that many were killed in this action and that Cato in his history the *Origines* wrote at length and with considerable verve about his own exploits and contribution to this victory.

> He says that those who saw him pursuing and cutting down the enemy felt that Rome owed more to Cato than he to his city, and that the consul Manius himself, flushed with victory threw his arms around Cato in a long embrace and cried aloud in sheer joy that neither he nor the entire Roman people could ever repay Cato for his services to the state.   (Plut., *Cato the Elder*, 14)[12]

Although Antiochus lost some more of his teeth he escaped to fight another day as probably did a fair section of his army returning to Demetrias and its impregnable fortifications. However, Livy using Polybius has this to say:

> No one escaped from the entire army except for the five hundred who were the king's body guard, and also a small number of the ten thousand who, we have written on the authority of Polybius, crossed with the king into Greece.   (Livy, 36.19.11)

This is probably further misrepresentation by Livy, although Appian (*Syr.* 4.20) concurs with the figure of 10,000 casualties on the Syrian side which accounts for the entire infantry composition of his invasion force. Antiochus, in defeat, certainly true to form retreated as far as possible from the front line, first to Elateia, then Chalcis and then abandoning Euboea altogether and not risking a further engagement with the Romans until he could call upon his entire army. He sailed for Ephesus with his new bride.

Those Greeks in Phocis and on the island of Euboea who had supported Antiochus quickly made their peace with the Romans, but Aetolia was subject to a serious attack by Glabrio and Philip V, and the Aetolian League general Democritus was captured. This same Democritus is reputed to have hubristically threatened the Romans with a war on their own doorstep (App., *Syr.* 4.21). Yet the Aetolian League was defeated within barely a single campaigning season; always more bluff than substance, the Aetolians were finished as a power block in Greece. On the other hand, Philip was rewarded for his services by having his eldest son Demetrius, who had been taken as a hostage for Macedonian good behaviour, returned to him (App., *Syr.* 4.20).

Antiochus even at this late stage had several options worth exploiting since he held both sides of the Hellespont, and commanded a fleet at least as powerful as the Romans. Over the fleet, which was clearly augmented at this stage (App., *Syr.* 4.21), he placed the Rhodian exile, perhaps a mercenary, Polyxenidas.[13] At the same time he returned to Thrace strengthened the fortifications of Sestos and Abydos which commanded the Hellespont, and made Lysimacheia his base of operations and accumulated supplies of all necessities for the war there.

Meanwhile, Livius Salinator was placed in command of a Roman fleet of eighty-one warships and was joined by fifty more from Pergamum commanded by its king Eumenes II.[14] This fleet sailed into the harbour of Phocaea, nominally Syrian, but which allowed them access out of fear of siege and the threat of destruction. On the next day the Roman commander looked for his opposing number. Polyxenidas was nearby and ready to engage with a fleet comprising 200 ships but of the smaller more agile variety. Two Punic ships on the Roman side sailed out of line and were captured by three Syrian vessels though their crews swam away to safety. Salinator is said to have sailed his own ship against the three Syrians which grappled his with hooks and, tied together, a land fight developed on the ships. The Romans of course were larger with a greater number of soldiers on board and so were able to overcome their opponents who lost two of their ships. The rival fleets then came together as a general melee took place in which the Syrian fleet came off worse but, since the Roman ships and those of their allies were the more cumbersome, the enemy was able to escape complete destruction by racing off to Ephesus. Salinator led his fleet into Chios where he was joined by further reinforcements from Rhodes amounting to another twenty-seven ships, giving him by that stage in excess of 150 ships. The fleet of Polyxenidas had obviously suffered some losses since the king ordered Hannibal to Syria to oversee the equipping of a new fleet from Cilicia and Phoenicia, but he was then blockaded in Pamphylia with this force by another Rhodian detachment (App., *Syr.* 5.22).

The new consul Lucius Cornelius Scipio took command of Glabrio's army in Aetolia. He, and his elder brother Scipio Africanus, who was present as a member of the general's staff, decided to leave the reduction of any recalcitrant towns for the time being. Instead they aimed to take the war to Antiochus as quickly as they could so if possible to complete the campaign before Lucius' term of command expired.[15] The Roman army marched north through Macedonia and into Thrace, a route made easier by the cooperation of Philip who had ordered the repair of roads and bridges, offered supplies and guards and entertained the commanders.[16] Prusias, the king of Bithynia, was also offered an advantageous treaty if he joined with the Romans against Antiochus and he readily agreed to this. In conjunction with this advance the naval commander Livius Salinator moved north leaving the Rhodian Pausimachus in charge of a substantial squadron to cover the south Aegean. There was little opposition to the Roman-Pergamene fleet from the Hellespontine cities, which including Phocaea, Samos, Sestos and Rhoeteum changed their allegiance. However, Abydos remained in Syrian hands and was besieged.

Pausimachus is said (App., *Syr.* 5.24) to have spent time training his crews until he was lured into a trap by Polyxenidas who promised him Antiochus' fleet in return for allowing him to return to Rhodes. Pausimachus suspected treachery but a signed letter from Polyxenidas and the fact that the Syrian fleet had moved out from Ephesus and had dispersed looking for supplies caused the former to allow his guard to drop, and he ordered his own fleet to do likewise. Polyxenidas saw his plan progressing and sent Nicander, a Cilician pirate, over to Samos with instructions to attack the rear of the Roman fleet which had beached for the night. Polyxenidas himself sailed overnight and attacked at dawn. The battle took place on the beach, as was often the case with ancient naval engagements, as Pausimachus first abandoned his ships and then in the confusion caused by the attack from inland tried to regain them.[17] He was killed in the fighting, and most of his fleet was captured and towed into Ephesus. The victory gave a respite to the Syrian cause as Phocaea and Samos again changed sides. Livius Salinator then returned from the Hellespont with contingents from Pergamum and Rhodes and arrived outside Ephesus and offered battle. Polyxenidas did not venture out seeing that the disparity in size of warships still remained. A part of the Roman fleet landed troops to plunder the coast but were driven off by Nicander, and so the entire fleet withdrew to Samos into winter quarters as Salinator's term of command came to an end.[18]

At the start of the next spring Antiochus' son Seleucus invaded Pergamum and besieged the city which caused Eumenes to leave his naval duties with the Romans and return to his capital. He was accompanied by L. Aemilius Regillus, Livius Salinator's successor.[19] The Achaean League, says Appian (*Syr.* 5.26), had also sent 1,000 infantry and 100 cavalry commanded by a certain Diophanes. When he observed the Syrian troops at leisure beneath the walls of Pergamum he urged a sally, but the Pergamenes refused. So he led out his own small force which was at first ignored by the enemy, but then he attacked while they were taking their dinner and caused chaos killing a large number and capturing some prisoners. Next day he led his troops out again and this time Seleucus lined up his cavalry and invited an attack but Diophanes refused to be drawn. Finally Seleucus decided to retire in order that his own force could take their meal and take care of their horses, at which point the Achaeans attacked again causing mayhem. In the next days, Diophanes apparently continued his unorthodox tactics to the delight of the locals, who did not join him, but he brought the invaders such discomfort that they withdrew not only from the city but beyond the kingdom's territory. The capture of Pergamum was probably never really a feasible objective given its fortifications but to have kept Eumenes engaged here and not allowing him to provide the Roman with logistical support would have increased the chances of Antiochus achieving a favourable outcome in the war. This was a serious reverse and should have indicated to the king that his options were becoming limited. Of course we are not told the size or calibre of Seleucus' forces and it may well be that a stronger and better organised attack would have produced the required result. Again it does look as if poor command was at fault on the Syrian side and allowed the Romans a further psychological advantage without them having to do very much themselves.

At sea, near the town of Myonessus, matters also took a turn for the worse for the Syrian king. The Roman fleet, now consisting of eighty-three decked ships, including twenty-five from Rhodes, took on the Syrian fleet of ninety decked ships still commanded by Polyxenidas.[20] The Seleucids' left wing began a *periplous* or encircling action extending their wing beyond that of the Roman right but this was noticed by the Rhodian commander Eudorus on the Roman left wing. He brought his ships behind the line to strengthen the Roman right wing and also employed fire ships to good effect. The Seleucid ships shied away from the fire hazard, but were forced into difficult avoidance manoeuvres, and as a result some sustained damage to their prows and others took water.

> Finally a Rhodian ship rammed one from Sidon, and the impact was so great that the latter's anchor became dislodged and stuck in the former so that they were joined together. The two ships lay not moving and the fight between the two crews became like a land battle. As many others joined the cause of each side the fight became a crucial one until the Romans broke through the centre of Antiochus which had been weakened by the fight and surrounded the enemy before they realised it. (App., *Syr.* 5.27)

With that came attempted flight, chaos among the defeated, and the pursuit of those escaping. The defeat was not a complete annihilation, but was a serious reverse with the loss of roughly a third of the Syrian fleet while the Romans lost just two of their ships and the Rhodians one.[21] The Syrians had the financial capability, resources and know-how to rebuild and retrain crews, but they needed time.[22] And time was beginning to run out. Indeed, panic is said to have struck the king, and he squandered any advantages he possessed to instead place his future fortunes on the outcome of a single land battle.

Without any defence of Lysimacheia being attempted, and without the Roman army even in sight, when he heard the news of the defeat at Myonnessus, Antiochus abandoned the city without a fight leaving all its valuable stores to the Romans who were still advancing from Thrace. So disorganized was the retreat that not only was the Thracian side surrendered but the crossing too was left unguarded and Abydos which had remained loyal to the king was also forgotten. The Romans crossed the Hellespont unhindered, and the Scipios must have considered that the fortunes of war were certainly with them. In fact they were in Pergamum before Antiochus knew that they were in Asia. His intelligence network seems to have been either particularly inefficient or had simply collapsed, or Antiochus refused to listen or consult reports brought to him. Indeed, his temperamental nature plunged him into the depths of uncertainty and depression to such an extent that he sent an envoy to the Romans requesting a peace. His representative, Heraclides of Byzantium, was instructed to offer to give up Smyrna, Alexandria-on-the-Granicus, and Lampsacus which had been a source of contention between Rome and Syria. Heraclides was also empowered to offer to pay half the costs of the war and if pressed to release any Ionian or Aeolian cities which had sided with Rome from obligations to the king and to obey any other demand made by the Scipios. He was also given the authority if in private discussions with the Scipios to offer a large bribe and to promise the release of Africanus' son who had recently been captured at sea between Chalcis and Demetrias.[23] In private Africanus is said to have told Heraclides that, had the king held Lysimacheia or even the Asian side of the Hellespont when he opened negotiations, his peace offers would have been enthusiastically accepted; as it was the official response was as follows.

> If Antiochus wishes peace he must surrender not only the cities of
> Ionia and Aeolia, but all of Asia this side of Mount Taurus, and he
> must pay the costs of the entire war   (App., *Syr.* 29)

Africanus is said to have privately thanked the king for his kind offer to return his son, and advised Antiochus to accept these terms rather than place his chances on an uncertain future.

At this point we are told that Africanus was taken ill and he stayed at Elaia, the port for Pergamum, while his brother continued the campaign against Antiochus. However, Livy (37.37) states that the king was advised by Africanus that he should delay giving battle to the Romans until he himself had recovered from his illness and was present again with his brother Lucius. His account of the preliminary events leading to the battle is therefore to be placed in quite a different context to that of Appian. The king originally had a camp near Thyateira (the modern town of Akhisar) and although credited by Livy with an army of 60,000 infantry and 12,000, such was his respect for Africanus that:

> He withdrew, crossing the Phrygius River and made a camp close
> to Magnesia-ad-Sipylum. Meanwhile the consul believing that
> Antiochus was still at Thyateira advanced by forced marches ...
> when he found that the king had gone he followed along the course
> of the Phrygius and made his camp about four miles from his enemy.

The Romans, therefore, almost certainly marched from Pergamum up to the headwaters of the Caicus River and from there down into the valley of the Phrygius River (also called the Hyllus) as far as its confluence with the Hermus River, quite close to Magnesia-ad-Sipylum. For about a week there was heavy skirmishing between the two sides, that of Antiochus generally being worsted in these engagements. Then the Romans crossed the Phrygius, intent on making their camp even closer to the Seleucid encampment, which had extensive fortifications. Lucius Scipio, the consul, was keen to give battle while his term of command remained and winter conditions were imminent. A further advance towards the Seleucid camp was ordered; this time Antiochus, concerned in case his army's morale would suffer if he continued to decline battle, ordered his own forces to assemble and meet the Romans. The king had evidently remained to be convinced that another bout of fighting would not harm his future, indeed whether he won or lost, even waiting for the return of Africanus.[24]

The consul, who played an oddly passive role in this whole episode, first deferred to his elder brother but then to another ambitious *novus homo*, Gnaeus Domitius Ahenobarbus, his senior legate or staff officer, who was very anxious to engage Antiochus as quickly as possible.[25] It was Ahenobarbus who was instrumental in seeing that Romans crossed the Phrygius, clearly not to be deterred from action, and establishing a camp a mere 20 stades (4,040 yards or rather less than 4 kilometres) from that of Antiochus. For the next four days each side drew up their armies in front of their respective camps but neither made the first moves to open the engagement. On day five Domitius ordered an advance but the Seleucid army refused the challenge, and the Romans moved their camp even closer. Antiochus still wanted to avoid a battle until Africanus came back from Elaia, although he found it very difficult to resist the temptation of battle; and now Domitius sent heralds to the walls of the Syrian camp to announce that he would do battle on the next day whether his opponents were willing to or not. Antiochus could still have simply held his fort or repelled the Romans from outside his walls but instead he chose, after probably not much hesitation and in keeping with adherence to his warrior ethos, took up the challenge offered by the Romans.

On the next morning at dawn both armies were arranged.[26] Appian says that the Romans had 10,000 legionaries on their left wing at the bank of the river. Next to these were 10,000 infantry from the Italian allies. Each of these essentially heavy infantry brigades were lined up three deep. A slightly smaller contingent made up of Pergamene troops, mainly heavy cavalry, and light infantry or peltasts from the Achaean League made up the right wing. Added to this Domitius had numerous other lightly armed troops – slingers, bowmen – and four *alae* or troops of cavalry. Lucius Scipio took command of the centre, Domitius the right wing, and Eumenes the left wing. In total the Roman army numbered roughly 30,000.[27] On the face of it the Seleucid army was far superior in number since it is said to have totalled 70,000 men (App., *Syr.* 6.31). In the centre of the line was a 16,000-strong Macedonian phalanx equipped with the sarissa, first employed by Philip II and then by Alexander the Great. The phalanx had to be deep for the momentum to build as the troops rushed forward and carry it forward against and ideally through an opponent's heavy infantry. Hence there were ten sections along the centre with a front line of fifty in each section and a depth of thirty-two in each.[28] The Macedonian phalanx, as all phalanx formations, was highly susceptible to attack from the rear since the phalangites wore little armour, and if their charge proved ineffective they became vulnerable, as events had proved at Cynoscephalae just seven years before. Its flanks therefore needed to be well protected, and in this instance twenty-five elephants on each side provided some protection.

> The appearance of the phalanx was very much like a wall of which the elephants were the towers.   (App., *Syr.* 6.32)

Livy gives a somewhat more detailed account of the armies as they paraded

> There were two legions of Roman citizens and two of Latin allies each with a total of 5,400 men. The Romans occupied the centre, and each of the Latin legions holding the wings: in the front line were the *hastati*, next the *principes*, and in the rear the *triarii*. The consul positioned on the right wing, outside the main or regular formation for battle, on a line with the legions, Eumenes' contingent made up of about 1,000 Achaean light armed troops. Beyond these he stationed the cavalry in total 3,000 about 800 of whom were provided by Eumenes, the rest Roman. Finally on this flank he placed contingents of about 500 each from Tralles and Crete. Since the left wing was protected by the river and its steep banks it did not need to be protected by auxiliary troops but four cavalry units were placed here by the consul. This was the composition of the Roman army, but as a guard for the camp there were also 2,000 Macedonian and Thracian mercenaries.
>
> The king's army was more varied since it contained many ethnic groups who used different weapons and auxiliary troops. There were 10,000 infantry called phalangites armed in the fashion of the Macedonians, which made up the centre. Their front was divided into ten units each separated from one another and in each of the intervening gaps two elephants were positioned. The depth of the

phalanx from front to back was thirty-two ranks. This was the main strength of the king's army, presenting an intimidating appearance more so because of the elephants. On the right wing of the phalanx the king stationed 1,500 Galatian infantry and next to these 3,000 cataphracts or heavily armoured cavalry.   (Livy, 37.39–40)

He goes on to add all the numerous units which made Antiochus' right wing: 1,000 Median cavalry, the king's own bodyguard the 'Silver Shields' or *argyraspides*, mounted archers, light-armed troops from Tralles and Crete (curiously on both sides), archers and slingers, totalling altogether about 12,000 men. On the left wing a further 1,500 Galatian infantry was stationed with a contingent from Cappadocia numbering 2,000. Beyond this section came a mixture of units, amounting to at least 15,000 troops but of some uncertain value, consisting of Syrian and Phrygian cataphracts, Arab archers mounted on camels, conventional cavalry, scythed chariots and other light-armed troops, not to mention a further troop of 16 elephants.

Antiochus had obviously stationed predominantly cavalry troops on each wing, and he evidently believed that this capability was his trump card against a mainly-infantry opposition. In equal numbers, says Appian, heavily armoured Galatian cavalry and Macedonian horse were stationed on the wings. In amongst these on the right wing were other lighter-armed horsemen and some mounted archers, while on the left wing there were a number of Gallic levies and some Cappadocians which had been provided by their king Ariarathes. Besides these there were also other infantry and cavalry troops from Asia Minor and as far afield as Arabia: javelin throwers, archers – infantry and cavalry, peltasts and slingers. There were also scythed chariots to be placed out in front in advance of the Syrian line to begin the battle but to retire once hostilities started in earnest. On paper it seems a formidable line-up but there were serious flaws in Antiochus' plans: scythed chariots were never very effective in battle, and elephants could be more of a problem for their own side than the enemy, but much more serious was that the possible vulnerability of the phalanx was clearly ignored. Again Appian notes that the centre was by far the most disciplined and well-trained section of the army, yet it was deployed in a narrow space (App., *Syr.* 6.32), quite unsuitable for it to be fully effective.[29] Perhaps indeed Antiochus was mindful of the result at Cynoscephalae and sought to limit the engagement of his heavy infantry and trust instead to the weight of his cavalry charge. The king took command of the right wing, and his son Seleucus the left; Philip, master of the elephants, commanded in the centre, while Mendis and Zeuxis (the latter one of Antiochus' closest and most senior counsellors) were responsible for starting the proceedings.[30]

The morning in December 190 proved to be a dull and misty one, and probably quite cool. The array from the opposing armies hardly glittered and the mist appears to have reduced the efficacy of the skirmishers and their use of slings and other missiles. However, the scythed chariots were soon on the move mainly directed against the Roman right wing and Eumenes. Ever since Alexander's encounters with these armoured cars of ancient Asian armies, the most effective way of dealing with them was either to avoid them completely and let them run through gaps in the lines and then shoot at the drivers' backs, or to disable the engines, in other words, the horses. This is what Euemenes ordered his men to do: to strike at the horses which once injured would run amok among their own side or make their drivers easy targets for the infantry. And this is indeed what occurred. The squadrons of chariots dissolved into chaos, Arabian mounted archers on camels were likewise thrown into a disordered mess and next to these some of the heavy armoured cataphracts were also severely distracted by the task in hand. It is interesting to note that the use of these chariots, like the use of elephants, had continued even in the face of the obvious risks to their users. Panic caused by this chaos and disorder spread among the ranks on the Syrian left wing which then had to bear the brunt of a rapid advance by Eumenes' cavalry, which broke the enemy causing heavy losses as the cataphracts were unable to turn while other horsemen simply fled. This reverse cost the phalanx its left side protection now open to attack from the Roman right wing.

Meanwhile, Antiochus leading the attack on the right, the offensive, wing of his army seems to have rapidly broken through the Roman line and pursued some of the infantry or cavalry here. The account here is much less specific and it may be that the Romans deliberately let the king through. It is notable that once again, as at Raphia nearly thirty years before, the king instead of attacking his opponents' centre from the rear instead galloped off in his usual un-disciplined fashion from the field in pursuit of fugitives – great bravado but of little use when a more vital coordination of his forces was needed. Perhaps he had great confidence in his son and his other senior generals, but he can also be soundly condemned for leaving his centre open to attack on its right now as well as its left. And indeed the phalanx which, says Appian, should have been the most effective part of the Seleucid army because of its training and formidable discipline, was surrounded by Eumenes leading his cavalry from the Roman right wing and Domitius Ahenobarbus from the Roman left, who does not appear to have been involved adversely by Antiochus' charge. Some prior planning may be evident here. The king's impetuous nature was by then well known and the Roman command may well have planned to lead him away from the battle in order to encircle his centre. And, although for a time the phalanx held its own in what became an orderly retreat, when the elephants which were in the midst of their ranks began to stampede crushing their own troops, the phalangites broke and ran for their lives. Many lost their lives in the rout.

> Thus crowded together in a rectangle, Domitius easily encircled them with his large numbers of cavalry and light-armed troops. Having no opportunity any longer to charge or to use the force of the mass the phalanx began to suffer severely. The soldiers were angry that they could not use their usual tactics while at the same time they were now exposed to the enemy's missiles. Still, they presented their densely packed sarissas on all four sides. The Romans did not come close or approach because they feared the discipline, the solid nature and the desperation of these experienced men. Instead they circled about hurling javelins and shooting off arrows none of which missed their mark in the densely packed crowd. The phalanx suffered severely and giving in to the situation they fell back slowly threatening the enemy and in perfect order and still a formidable fighting machine ... until the elephants inside the rectangle became excitable and unmanageable. It was only then that the phalangites broke and ran in flight.   (App., *Syr.* 6.35)

Therefore, when Antiochus returned from his pursuit he came across his shattered centre, destroyed left wing and Romans looting his own camp, realizing that the fight had gone against him, continued on his own flight to nearby Sardis, where he is supposed to have arrived at midnight. Even there he did not remain for long, however, and no thought was given for any further defence of Asia Minor, but only of retreat from any possible advance by the Roman army. Antiochus, with his wife and daughter, was soon at Apamea (also called Celaenae) where he was reunited with his son Seleucus. He then returned at once to Syria leaving his senior commanders to collect as many of his troops as remained alive. And he rapidly sent envoys to Lucius Scipio the consul to sue for an immediate peace on any terms. The Romans are said to have lost just twenty-four cavalry and 300 infantry, while Eumenes lost fifteen of his cavalry. The Seleucid army, on the other hand, was completely destroyed and even allowing for some exaggeration by the sources – Appian says perhaps as many as 50,000 killed with fifteen captured elephants – the death toll on the defeated side would have been high. Livy does not differ significantly from Appian in his estimation of casualties: Seleucid deaths, 50,000 infantry, 3,000 cavalry, 1,400 taken as prisoners, and the same number of captured elephants. The Romans the same number as given by Appian, twenty-four deaths among Eumenes' contingent (Livy 37.44.1).

Whichever way one looks at the result of this single engagement it was a disaster for Antiochus. This king may have grandiloquently liked to style himself *Megas* in imitation of Alexander, but as a general he hardly came close to true greatness since he committed cardinal and basic errors of judgement and leadership. He may have had some successes on the field of battle, notably in his campaigns in the east between 211 and 206, although we have few details and only Polybius' disparaging comments, and the noteworthy victory at Panion in 201; otherwise, his record is one of defeats: at Raphia in 217, Thermopylae in 191 and finally at Magnesia-ad-Sipylum in 190. He did not long survive this last calamity, dying a warrior's death on campaign, once again in the east, a little more than two years later.

Almost immediately after the battle ended the towns closest to the fight – Thyatira and Magnesia-ad-Sipylum – surrendered to the Romans. Sardis too within hours of the king's departure also sent envoys to the consul and ejected any Seleucid troops in the vicinity. Sardis in fact became the seat of the consul in a matter of days and from here he and his brother Africanus, who had recovered from his illness, conducted the peace treaty. The cities of Asia Minor in general very quickly abandoned any allegiance to Antiochus including Tralles, Magnesia-on Meander and Ephesus, the main Syrian naval base. Polyxenidas still in command of the Syrian fleet sailed south but unable to break the Rhodian blockade of Pamphylia abandoned his ships and went overland to Syria (Livy 37.45.1). Syrian power across the entire sub-continent vanished overnight.

Inexorably, the humiliation of peace was now imposed on Syria the vanquished by the victor rather than a settlement negotiated between equals. This arrangement has become known as the 'Peace of Apamea', which was ratified by the king and Roman senate in the year after the battle. Zeuxis, Antiochus' senior commander in Asia Minor, came to Sardis where he was received by the consul and his advisers, including Scipio Africanus. Livy records a speech delivered by Zeuxis in which on behalf of the king full responsibility for the war was acknowledged and that he had been wrong to wage this war against Rome and that his intermediary was there to gain a peace and forgiveness from the victors.

> With a magnanimous spirit you have always pardoned kings and nations you have conquered. In the hour of your victory which has made you the master of the world how much greater should that spirit be in deciding your actions, and how much more it would reflect greater on you to grant reconciliation. May you set aside any quarrels you have with mortal men and be like the gods and grant clemency and relief to the whole race of humans.
>
> (Livy 37.45.8–9)

Africanus had been designated to deliver the response:

> We Romans have those things that the immortal gods are
> empowered to grant. However, our feelings are controlled by our
> minds and these do not alter regardless of changing situations
> whether it is great success or in the worst adversity. As a witness to
> this as fact I could call on your friend Hannibal's evidence, notwith-
> standing others, if I was not able to call upon you. After we had
> crossed the Hellespont, before we saw the king's camp, before we
> saw his line of battle, when Mars, the god of war favoured neither
> side, and the outcome of the war was still in doubt, you sought peace.
> Then we offered to make a treaty as equals and now we offer these
> same terms as victors over the defeated. So keep out of Europe, with-
> draw from Asia this side of the Taurus Mountains. As indemnity for
> the war you must pay 15,000 Euboean talents, 500 now, 2,500 when
> the Roman senate and people have ratified the peace, and 1,000
> talents in annual instalments for the next twelve years. You must also
> compensate Eumenes and we have decided that you must pay him
> 400 talents and the wheat which was owed to his father. When we
> have agreed these terms and are assured that you will abide by them
> there will be a guarantee of this if you give us twenty hostages chosen
> by us. However, were will never be fully confident in your minds
> that the Roman people have obtained peace in any place where
> Hannibal remains so we demand his surrender unconditionally. So
> too we demand Thoas the Aetolian who was the prime mover of war
> ... Mnasilochus of Acarnania, and Philo and Eubulidas of Chalcis.
> The king now makes peace in a worse situation because he is later
> making it than he could have been. If he further delays let him be
> aware that it is more difficult to drag down the majesty of kings from
> the highest to the midway point than to cast it from that point to the
> bottom most depths.   (Livy 37.45.10–18)

The king's representatives had already been instructed to accept a peace at any
cost and so there was no need to carry on any further negotiations. A legation
was immediately sent to report the outcome of the war and terms of peace to
Rome even though it was now mid-December. The Romans billeted their
troops for the winter at Magnesia-on-Meander, Tralles and Ephesus. The
hostages were quickly brought to the consul at Ephesus together with a Syrian
delegation which also had to report to the senate. Eumenes also left for Rome as
did several other embassies from other cities and states in Asia Minor. The
Scipios had achieved their aim of concluding the war in a single if somewhat
extended campaigning season, with the climactic engagement actually taking

place outside what would once, but was no longer, the customary period of spring/summer fighting. Winter battles had become more common in the Hellenistic period, the use of mercenaries and semi-professional and later fully professional fighters meant that warfare was not dependent on the seasons. Fighting had become a year-long phenomenon and one which the Romans were fully able to exploit: in this instance to gain total control of the Mediterranean World.

Chapter 5

From Magnesia to the 'Asian Vespers'

Antiochus appeared to be not unduly distressed by his defeat at the hands of the Romans nor with the loss of 50,000 to his military capability, nor with the exacting tribute with which he was now faced and which surely caused financial distress to the cities in his empire and to his personal fortune. As a result one might have expected this wounded lion to go away and lick his wounds in solitude but such an action was simply not in keeping with this king's nature. He certainly returned to Antioch and true to the terms of his treaty with Rome, which was ratified by the senate, he never again crossed the Taurus Mountains.[1] However, it is also rather far-fetched to argue as Grainger does that Antiochus' action in making peace was one of 'great statesmanship' and that continuing to pursue the war after Magnesia might have embroiled the Romans in so difficult a campaign that they would have been forced to make a peace with Syria much more beneficial to the latter.[2] This projected outcome does not fit with the facts which were that Antiochus' crack hoplite phalanx had been utterly destroyed, his war fleet too had been left to burn on a beach in Asia Minor, and after this war he was short of funds. His eastern satrapies needed urgent attention and just possibly would provide him with the sort of situation where he might regain some of his battered prestige, acquire much needed wealth and train a new army – if indeed he ever indulged in such long term strategies. In the event we shall never know since Antiochus was killed in some petty fighting in 187. By then he was in his mid-fifties, his reign had lasted thirty-five years, he had been the most effective ruler of this kingdom since Seleucus its founder, yet his own abilities in every respect are questionable and his greatest moment was at Panion in 200; for the most part his rule was one of setbacks and defeats.

His successor Seleucus IV was his second son, since his eldest son Antiochus had died four years before the battle of Magnesia.[3] Seleucus had spent time at Rome as a hostage immediately after this debacle but had been allowed to return home. According to Appian (*Syr.* 66) Seleucus was an ineffectual ruler who was undoubtedly hampered in his ability to rule by the enfeebled kingdom's state caused by his father's defeat by the Romans. After his murder by a courtier named Heliodorus in 175, his brother styled Antiochus IV succeeded him. Antiochus had replaced his elder brother as hostage and so had been at

Rome for a number of years. His succession was promoted by Eumenes of Pergamum who preferred Antiochus to Seleucus' son Demetrius, who by then had become the latest Syrian princely hostage in Rome. Antiochus was certainly made of sterner stuff than his brother and soon led an invigorated kingdom to triumphs against Armenia, in Judaea, and especially against Egypt which he invaded in 169. Taking advantage of infighting among the royal family to which he was closely connected by blood, he marched to the Nile, occupied Memphis and the young king Ptolemy VI put himself in his uncle's hands.[4] Antiochus then marched to Alexandria, but the population spurred on by Ptolemy's sister and younger brother refused to surrender and so the Syrian king was obliged to withdraw from the Delta, probably because he lacked siege equipment and supplies for a protracted campaign. In his absence Ptolemy made peace with his siblings, which gave the Syrian monarch an excuse to launch a second campaign in the following year. Livy (45.11.4) tells us that the Syrians already had a garrison at Pelusium, which made the crossing of the Nile an easy matter to accomplish, and marched without opposition to Eleusis about four miles or roughly seven kilometres from Alexandria. There he met a delegation from Rome, including the former consul Gaius Popillius Laenas, with whom the king appears to have been on quite familiar terms.[5] Thus Antiochus in quite an unorthodox manner for an oriental monarch went forward to greet the Romans and offered his right hand to this Roman ex-consul. Popillius Laenas however rebuffed this approach and instead delivered a written copy of a senatorial decree, which demanded that the king vacate Egypt immediately. The king's response was that he would consider the request with his counsellors at which point:

> Popillius ... drew a circle in the sand around the king with the walking stick he held in his hand and said, 'Before you step out of this circle give a response that I may take to the senate.' The king hesitated for a moment, astonished by the lack of subtlety in the order and said, 'I shall do what the senate requests.' Only then did Popillius extend his right hand to the king as to a friend and ally.
>
> (Livy 45.12.5–6)

As Scullard notes, a weakened Egypt was saved from conquest by the Romans who forced Antiochus into a humiliating retreat at precisely the same time they had defeated at Pydna Perseus the last king of Macedonia and had abolished his kingdom: all events which further emphasised Rome's supremacy in the Mediterranean.[6] From this time on Seleucid Syria was no further problem to the Romans who, however, at least on one occasion interfered in the internal affairs of the kingdom to their advantage. After the death of Antiochus IV in 164 his young son was proclaimed as Antiochus V, although at Rome

Demetrius, the son of Seleucus IV by then about twenty-two years of age, requested that he should be recognised as king instead. The senate sent an embassy headed by Gnaeus Octavius which was intended to illustrate Roman approval for the new king, but also to order the destruction of a number of warships and elephants which the Syrians had maintained in excess of the treaty made with Antiochus III after Magnesia.[7] When Octavius was killed in a riot in Antioch Demetrius managed to escape his captivity and not only return to Syria but once there found he had enough support to overturn the government and have his cousin murdered. The Romans sent another delegation which confirmed the new king in his position. It was probably quite apparent to contemporaries – it is certainly evident with hindsight – that following the death of Antiochus IV, and within just twenty-five years of Magnesia, Seleucid Syria, like Ptolemaic Egypt, had ceased to be a world power.[8]

In Asia Minor Roman control had also tightened perceptibly especially during and after the war against Perseus (171–168). Macedonia ceased to be an independent state, first parcelled up into four separate republics and after the revolt of Andriscus between 149 and 148, the former kingdom was combined with mainland Greece into the Roman province of Achaea. Across the Aegean no permanent Roman presence was yet in place but through treaties between Rome and the various states in the region, any freedom of action without Roman approval became virtually impossible. At the same time friends and allies of Rome were increasingly scrutinised as to the extent of their trust and loyalty. Rhodes is a case in point. A strong supporter of Rome during the Second Macedonian War (201–197) and the war against Antiochus III (191–189) it had reaped the benefits of supplying the Romans with warships to control the Aegean and eastern Mediterranean. In the treaty of Apamea of 189, the Lycian cities and much of the hinterland in the south-west of Asia Minor including southern Caria were granted to the Rhodians,[9] confirming the city as the economic hub of the eastern Mediterranean. However, its acquisition of wealth also proved its undoing since a pro-Macedonian faction gradually gained power over the next twenty years. These politicians saw themselves as power brokers between Macedonia and the Romans, and were behind the move to send a legation to Rome to argue for a political accommodation between the two in 168. These miscalculated their arrival which occurred after the Roman victory at Pydna and misjudged senatorial attitudes which regarded such a role as inconsistent with that of an ally. The same Roman embassy sent to turn back Antiochus IV from Alexandria also called at Rhodes where its people were left in no doubt about Roman anger. The Rhodians responded by putting on trial and executing any public figure known to have favoured Perseus, but even this extreme reaction was not enough; and some politicians in the senate wanted an immediate war against the island state. A delegation to Rome in 167 gained no assurances of a permanent peace and for two more years Rome kept the Rhodians in a state of anxiety about their future. Then the Romans stripped Rhodes of its mainland possessions and made the island of Delos a free port which could henceforth compete with Rhodian shipping, its main industry, on an advantageous footing and so cause economic ruin. The severity of Rome's reaction to Rhodes possibly exhibits yet again exasperation and disgust at the way the ancient Greek states had a habit of switching allegiances at breakneck speed, but also points – though there is nothing said about this in the literary evidence – to real evidence of Rhodian complicity in the designs of Perseus. Rhodes did recover its position to some extent, and sent a flotilla of warships to join the Roman siege of Carthage in 149–146, but it was more than 200 years (AD 46) before its privileged status was restored by the emperor Claudius.

> He deprived the Lycians of their independence because of deadly internal feuding and restored the freedom of the Rhodians since they regretted their ancient faults.   (Suet., *Claud.* 25)

Pergamum too was initially well rewarded for its support against Philip V and Antiochus, especially for the role of its king Eumenes II in the victory at Magnesia-ad-Sipylum; and he was established as the Rome's watchdog in Asia, and as its main ally situated between Macedonia and Syria. Eumenes II was rewarded with territorial gains which greatly enlarged his kingdom which now consisted of not only the old Pergamene lands, but also adjacent possessions in Phrygia, Lydia as far south as parts of Lycia and Pisidia, and inland Pamphylia. But again during the war with Perseus, the Romans became highly suspicious about the ambitions of Eumenes. He too offered to mediate between Rome and Perseus in 168 by which time nothing less than total conquest had become the consensus aim of the Roman senate. Eumenes may have had good intentions but his action was seen as meddling in affairs which should not have concerned him. He evidently felt that his position was so under threat that he set out to Rome to explain his actions to the senate in person. He reached Italy where he was however ordered to return home and, although no further action was taken against him before his death in 158, he never regained Rome's trust. His brother who became Attalus II, co-ruler from 160 and king in 158, was urged by supporters at Rome to take power by a coup, but he refused. Once he was king he was able to restore his kingdom's position as a close ally of Rome and indeed was supported by the Romans in border wars with Bithynia and inter-fered, with Roman complicity, in the internal affairs of Syria, supporting the usurper Alexander Balas against Demetrius I in 150 (Polyb., 3.5). He also sent troops to join the Roman campaigns against Andriscus, between 149 and 148, and was on friendly terms with Scipio Aemilianus, the eventual destroyer of

Carthage.[10] On the death of Attalus II in 138 his nephew, the son of Eumenes II, became king. Diodorus (34/35.3.1) states that the new king was something of a despot and did not emulate his benign predecessor, but his reign was brief, he died young and heirless in 133 leaving his kingdom to Rome in his will. Rome, therefore, acquired its first province east of the Aegean Sea through a bequest and not by conquest.

There was immediate controversy about this gift to Rome which included some of the wealthiest cities of the Mediterranean, Pergamum itself with its famous library, but also the port of Ephesus and Sardis, formerly the capital of the Persian satrapy of Lydia.[11] Almost immediately there was a rebellion against the prospect of Roman rule which took hold since at Rome there was a domestic crisis caused by the legislation of Ti. Gracchus and because Roman armies were involved in a protracted war in Spain and a serious slave revolt in Sicily. The tribune of the plebs Gracchus had recently passed a law which would see public land allocated to citizens who had, in some way or other, lost their farms. The measure was certainly aimed at removing an unstable urban element and making these new landowners eligible for service in the army. The senate had initially supported the law but opponents of Gracchus now blocked its further implementation by denying funding to the commission which had been established to supervise the allocation of these new allotments. When Gracchus heard the unexpected news of the windfall from Asia Minor he immediately summoned the people and asked them to pass a law allowing the income from the new province to be used to finance his land law (Plut., *Ti. Gracchus*, 14.1–2). Gracchus was killed in a riot soon after but his law remained in force although it must be said that how it functioned is impossible to grasp since no sooner had it been proposed that the financing of his scheme be underwritten by Pergamene money than a certain Aristonicus proclaimed himself Eumenes III.[12]

Although the rebels were not supported by the vast majority of the cities and many of the people in Pergamum, and indeed only the city of Phocaea joined the cause willingly, there were initial successes, which is surprising since the neighbouring states of Cappadocia, Pontus and Bithynia all remained true to their treaties with Rome. A Roman army arrived in Pergamum only in 131 commanded by the consul Publius Licinius Crassus Mucianus, probably comprising two legions plus auxiliary troops.[13] No doubt the allied kings of Asia Minor were expected to supply additional forces especially in cavalry. More remarkable was the death of Mucianus caught in an ambush some-where between Smyrna and Elaia, the port for Pergamum, probably not by Aristonicus but by some bandits says Strabo (14.1.38; cf. Frontin., *Str.* 4.5.16). The following year another consul, M. Perperna, was sent out to take up the command and again not far from Pergamum met the rebels in battle where

Aristonicus was badly beaten and taken prisoner.[14] However, Perperna died soon after the battle from natural causes. M'. Aquillius, who was consul in 129, was sent out to terminate any remaining hostilities, and to oversee the start of the process of implementing a Roman administration. In order to accomplish that task a senatorial commission of ten was despatched to assess the amount of tribute from the new province and the various cities. So complex must this financial calculation have been and on such a massive scale, for the Romans had never occupied so wealthy a region before, that it will have taken several years to complete. Hence the Gracchan land commission sitting in Rome can hardly have utilized a vast reservoir of funds for its work.[15]

The absorption of Cilicia into the Roman Empire, only the second province east of the Hellespont did not occur for another twenty-five years; and its conquest became imperative not because of any interstate rivalry but because of the scourge of piracy. In the Treaty of Apamea, Antiochus III had been required to withdraw beyond the Taurus, but had been allowed to retain Cilicia Pedias, east of the Sarpedon Promontory which consisted of settled and agriculturally rich land including the prosperous city of Tarsus. Cilicia Tracheia to the west was left self-governing but, due to the mountainous nature of the land and isolated inlets, soon became a safe haven for ancient pirates in much the same way that the island of Tortuga in the Caribbean was for the seventeenth-century English and French buccaneers. Neither the Seleucids nor the Rhodians policed these waters any more and Ptolemaic fleets once common here seldom ventured beyond Cyprus. The Roman policy of weakening both potential and past rivals proved to be short-sighted and had the effect of allowing another sort of menace to flourish completely out of control. In a rather belated response the Romans sent M. Antonius, a praetor in 102, with a fleet to bring this region, referred to as the province of Cilicia, into some sort of order.[16] This was however clearly not a provincial command linked to a specific region such as Asia or Macedonia but rather a roving command in pursuit of the pirates wherever they might be encountered in these parts. Antonius appears to have had access to supplies from across Asia Minor according to Cicero (*Verr.* 2.1.95). He had some success too since the region of Tracheia was formally made a provincial command to be commanded by a praetor; and one of its first incumbents was Lucius Cornelius Sulla, perhaps in 97 or 96,[17] who was to play such a major role in the next wars in Asia Minor and in the affairs of state as a whole. Still with a civil war in Italy starting in 91 Cilician and the affairs of Asia Minor were largely forgotten at Rome, a situation which played into the hands of a far greater foe than the pirates and which began with a systematic act of genocide the equivalent of the Sicilian Vespers.

Chapter 6

Mithridates VI Eupator: The First War

In 98 BC Gaius Marius, recently victorious against the Germanic tribes the Cimbri and Teutones, made a trip to Galatia in order to give personal thanks to the Great Mother (*Magna Mater* a personification of the goddess Demeter) at Pessinus in fulfilment of promises he had made while in command of the campaigns in southern Gaul and northern Italy. When he was in Galatia he is said to have met King Mithridates VI Eupator of Pontus. Plutarch, in his life of Marius (*Mar.* 31.1–3), gives an account of this encounter and reasons behind the meeting.

> What he (Marius) hoped was to stir up trouble among the rulers of Asia especially to incite Mithridates who was believed to be about to make war on Rome. Marius would then immediately be granted the command against him and would be able to bring delight to the Romans with the spectacle of more triumphs ... when Mithridates treated him extremely politely and with due respect Marius was not impressed and said merely 'Either endeavour to be stronger than the Romans, King, or else remain silent and do as you are told.'

The king, says Plutarch, was astonished with this advice having heard of Roman bluntness but never before having been on its receiving end. It is impossible to judge the historical accuracy of such an interview, especially when Plutarch interweaves Marius' greed for more personal glory, and it must be said an avaricious desire to further enrich himself, into this episode. It is of course possible that Marius did indeed meet Mithridates, and that the king of Pontus came on an official visit to one of Rome's most prominent living senators. It is unlikely, however, that this was the first time that Mithridates came across this form of Roman diplomacy.[1]

Mithridates succeeded to the throne of Pontus in about 120 when still a boy probably about fourteen years of age, and the government of the kingdom for the first four or five years was in the hands of his mother. She was finally suppressed when the king took on a more active role and so began a rule, which extended for over half a century, much of which brought the monarch into direct conflict with the Roman Empire. A vigorous warrior in the same vein as earlier Hellenistic rulers such as Philip V of Macedonia and Antiochus III of

Syria he soon led his armies in campaigns against neighbouring kings and particularly targeted the tribes and their lands along the eastern shores of the Black Sea, against whom he was triumphant. He was clearly intent on extending Pontic rule wherever this could be achieved long before his encounter with Marius. It was soon after this interview, perhaps as a way of gauging a Roman response that Mithridates began to interfere in the neighbouring kingdoms of Cappadocia and Bithynia. In 92 he was instructed by the senate to restore Ariobarzanes to the throne of Cappadocia whom he had recently deposed. Instead Mithridates attacked Bithynia expelled its king Nicomedes IV and installed in his place a brother of the monarch named Socrates, and although he first allowed Ariobarzanes back into Cappadocia, he then sent two generals Mithraas and Bagoas to expel him and proclaimed Ariarathes, probably one of his own sons, in his place.[2] The Roman response was to send a senior Roman senator, Manius Aquillius (consul in 101), in 89 to ensure the restoration of both allied kings and to that end he was to employ the small garrison based at Pergamum commanded by its governor L. Cassius Longinus. Mithridates, again ordered to comply with Roman demands, ignored the request, but he appears to have sat passively by while the former kings were reinstated by this small Roman force. The Romans then urged both kings to start hostilities against Pontus assuring them of support if they did so. Neither was enthusiastic knowing the power of Pontus but Nicomedes went so far as to raid Pontic territory up to the city of Amastris without encountering any opposition. His troops returned with a great deal of plunder, says Appian (*Mith.* 2.11), but had only been sent in the first place because the king of Bithynia was up to his neck in debt to the Romans so had little room for manoeuvre in this matter. Mithridates then sent an ambassador to Pergamum to complain of Nicomedes' actions and he received the following declaration:

> We would not want Mithridates to suffer any wrong done to him by Nicomedes, but we also cannot allow him to make war on Nicomedes because we consider that to be against Roman interest to have him weakened.   (App., *Mith.* 2.14)

The ambiguous nature of the reply to Mithridates' appeal for some sort of justice, although he was hardly free from blame himself, allowed him to set more belligerent actions into motion. He sent Ariarathes back to Cappadocia to expel Ariobarzanes. Mithridates then sent another legate to the Romans to announce and defend his action but at the same time leaving little doubt that he would no longer tolerate Roman interference in what he considered to be his sphere of influence. The Romans were suitably annoyed, as was intended, and they sent his legate packing. Then they levied troops without waiting for sanction from Rome and attempted to invade Pontus in three columns, the first commanded by Cassius Longinus who took the route along the border between Bithynia and Galatia, another led by Aquillius who went directly through Bithynia and the third by Quintus Oppius, governor of Cilicia, via Cappadocia. Appian states that altogether this invasion force amounted to about 200,000 infantry and cavalry, composed mainly of raw levies from the allied states, Bithynia foremost among them. Mithridates responded by putting an army of nearly 300,000 into the field which, like the Roman army was divided into various groups. One of these fought and beat the Bithynian troops of Nicomedes, a reverse which caused the whole Roman strategy to unravel: Nicomedes retreated to Pergamum, Aquillius headed for Rhodes, Cassius to Apamea (Celaenae) and Oppius – defeated at Laodicea on Lycus – was captured by Mithridates. The whole of western Asia Minor fell to the Pontic king without further fighting and Aquillius, captured on Lesbos, was brought to Pergamum and executed.[3] By this act, Mithridates proclaimed his future intentions and threw down the gauntlet!

Having occupied the Roman province of Asia, soon afterwards Mithridates ordered the murder of all Roman or Italian residents. It is said that 80,000 were killed by the inhabitants of cities such as Ephesus, Tralles, Pergamum and Adramyttium who were motivated by fear of, or enthusiasm for, the Pontic monarch who also evidently exploited local anti-Roman sentiments.[4] Large numbers of Romans and other Italians connected with commercial shipping or tax farming had taken up residence in the cities of the former kingdom of Pergamum and of Ionia.

> The people of Ephesus grabbed fugitives even when they had taken refuge in the temple of Artemis ... the people at Pergamum killed with arrows those who fled to the sanctuary of Aesculapius and were still clinging to his statues. The citizens of Adramyttium followed into the sea those trying to escape and drowned them. The people of Tralles, to avoid the crime of murder hired a savage named Theophilus of Paphlagonia to do the work. He led the victims to the temple of Concord and murdered them there.
>
> (App., *Mith.* 4.23)

Mithridates also launched an assault by sea on Rhodes, but failed to take the island which remained faithful to its alliance with Rome, besides accepting any Roman or Italian refugees who managed to escape the 'Asian Vespers' including Cassius Longinus, erstwhile governor of Asia. Still the Rhodians could do little but defend themselves since the king's timing was well chosen for the Romans, though they made a formal declaration of war on Pontus, were then actually involved in fierce fighting in Italy, and could spare no immediate help.

The desire for Roman citizenship by the elite of the Italian communities and continued prevarication on this issue by the senate finally led to an outbreak of civil war between the Romans and their Italian allies. The fighting was bitter and strongly contested. The Romans rapidly promised full citizenship rights to the people of Latium and Etruria and these as a result stayed largely loyal, but the hill tribes including the Samnites were a determined enemy well versed in Roman military matters and often a major component of the Empire's armies. Within a second campaigning season and with Roman victories in the field the senate conceded citizenship to all Italy south of the Rubicon and fighting for the most part ceased, although pockets of resistance to Rome continued in the far south and in Campania centred on the town of Nola.[5] Here the Roman general L. Cornelius Sulla who had shown great competence in the war, and prior to that his governorship of Cilicia, was in charge of the siege and was elected consul for 88.

A war against Mithridates was clearly looming and Sulla was assigned that task, but just at the point that an accommodation had been reached with the Italian allies and when a potentially disastrous situation for Rome had been turned around, the city itself was suddenly plunged into chaos. Publius Sulpicius, a tribune of the people, formerly an ally of the consuls fell out with them over the question of the registration of new citizens about which the highly conservative senate was dragging its heels. Clashes occurred in the Forum between supporters of the two sides, and the consuls were driven out of the city. The son of one of the consuls Q. Pompeius Rufus was killed and Sulla fled to his camp at Nola. Not long afterwards, Sulpicius proposed in an assembly that Gaius Marius be granted the command against Pontus instead of the consul. Any political issue was liable to scrutiny by the people in whose votes lay the ultimate decision. The allocation of the command to Sulla had been legally enacted but it could be overturned by a plebiscite.[6] It was perhaps a remarkable choice seeing that Marius was already nearly seventy years of age and had had limited successes in the war with the Italian allies and no other service in the army since his victories over the Germanic tribes over a decade before, but indicates the persuasive oratory of Sulpicius, certainly one of the most accomplished of his day, and his influence with the people. A majority of the senate, and the consuls, were perturbed by this move not least Sulla who refused to accept the decision. He persuaded his troops to march on the city and restore a government which he represented, more or less truthfully, as having been undermined and supplanted by a tribune and his influential backers. The soldiers, for the most part, levied from the citizen body, in its restricted pre-civil war sense, responded to his request with some gusto. However, most of Sulla's officer corps refused to be associated with what was a further rebellion against the state.[7] Only his quaestor L. Licinius Lucullus accompanied his commander from Nola, but there will have been many citizens of social and political standing among his six legions; and these were battle-hardened veterans.[8] The three thousand gladiators and numerous freed slaves employed by Sulpicius and Marius to defend the city stood no chance (Plut., *Sull.* 8.2).

> When it was informed that Sulla was marching on Rome, the senate sent two praetors – Brutus and Servilius – to order him to withdraw. These spoke rather harshly to Sulla and for this reason the soldiers broke up their *fasces*, tore off their uniforms of office and turned them out of the camp.[9]   (Plut., *Sull.* 9.2)

Two of Sulla's officers, appointed by him or among those who chose not to stand by, somehow took the gate and a section of the wall at the Esquiline Hill.[10] Sulla himself leading the main body was following closely so that in no time at all he had occupied a sector of the city without having to resort to siege tactics or indeed without incurring casualties. And it was only at this point that severe fighting began between the insurgents and the city population, not the supporters of Sulpicius and Marius, who seem strangely absent.

> Basilus and his men successfully forced their way into the city, but then their advance ground to a halt under a hail of stones and tiles thrown from the roofs by the unarmed people of the city and they withdrew to the wall. At that moment Sulla arrived and seeing what was happening ordered his men to fire the houses and was the first to do this after he had seized a torch. In the meantime, Marius was ... not able to check his enemy's advance and so fled from Rome.
>   (Plut., *Sull.* 9.5–7)

Sulla exacted revenge on his opponents including Sulpicius who was murdered while Marius escaped into exile. He also presided over the new consular elections attempting to oversee a result sympathetic to his cause. One of the new consuls, Octavius, seems to have accepted the fait accompli, but the intentions of the other, L. Cornelius Cinna, were far less certain. With the end of his year in office in sight Sulla set out with his assigned legions to tackle Mithridates.

The turmoil in Italy and then the unrest in Rome itself had given Mithridates the confidence to attack Greece and to add this Roman province to his acquisitions in Asia. So taking advantage of the troubles in Italy, Ariarathes, one of his sons, led an army across the Hellespont into Thrace to threaten Macedonia. One of Mithridates' generals Archelaus had used his fleet to gain control of much of the Aegean and had taken Euboea and Athens, from where he launched an attack northwards into Thessaly. At Chaeronea he was met by a

Roman force commanded by the quaestor Q. Bruttius Sura, despatched there by the governor of the province of Achaea, C. Sentius.[11] He defeated Archelaus in a hard-fought series of engagements forcing the Mithridatic army to retreat. At that point Sura was ordered to return to Macedonia by the quaestor Lucullus (Plut., *Sull.* 11.5), who announced Sulla's imminent arrival and who, of course, had command of the campaign. However, Sura's achievements meant that many of the cities of Greece preferred to side with Rome rather than with the invaders. The major exception here was Athens which had fallen under the control of Aristion an ally of Mithridates. Sulla's army entered Attica and Athens was besieged.

Plutarch's account is imprecise, but it seems to show that Sulla initially besieged the Piraeus and so prevented supplies from reaching the city which by then was no longer connected to its harbour by the famous long walls.[12] Sulla was in a hurry to gain a victory because events in Rome had taken a turn for the worse. The consul Cinna had first been driven out by his colleague and then had allied himself with Marius and together they had marched on Rome, taken the city easily then killed many of Sulla's friends and political allies, and declared Sulla a public enemy. Marius may still have coveted the Mithridatic command and became consul for a seventh time in January 86, but he died suddenly seventeen days later (Plut., *Mar.* 46.5). L. Valerius Flaccus was elected his replacement and sent to supersede Sulla and lead the war into Asia. Sulla wanted to return to Italy but first needed to reduce Athens and was desperate for money and supplies himself. He raided the treasuries of Delphi of their gold and silver, a sacrilegious action which can have gained him no friends in Greece, but which he needed to pay his troops.[13] He also requisitioned huge numbers of pack animals for the transportation of siege equipment with which to invest Athens more closely, and the surrounding countryside was denuded of trees in order to replace siege materials. The use of treasures dedicated to Apollo at Delphi to pay soldiers was of great concern to Plutarch who stresses the dangers of such a practice.[14]

> ... the generals of these later times were men who rose to promi-
> nence through violence rather than by merit and they needed their
> armies to fight against other generals more often than against an
> external threat, consequently they combined political strategies with
> the authority of a general. They spent money on making the lives of
> their soldiers easier and then after they had bought their support in
> this way they forgot to realise that they had put the state up for sale
> and had positioned themselves as slaves to the worst type of human-
> kind in order to rule the best. And it was Sulla who most set this
> example. In order to corrupt and win over the allegiance of soldiers

1. The Hellespont with Europe in the distance.
(*Author's photograph*)

2. The Hellespont near Dardanus, where the treaty of 84 BC was agreed.
(*Author's photograph*)

The coast near Myonessus, where the Romans defeated the fleet of Antiochus III. (*Author's photograph*)

4. The plain of the Hermus River near Magnesia-ad-Sipylum, modern Manisa.
(*Author's photograph*)

5. Mount Sipylum, close by the site of the battle between the Roman and Seleucid armies in December 190 BC.
(*Author's photograph*)

6. Sardis, to which Antiochus fled in the immediate aftermath of defeat at Magnesia. Seen here are the Temple of Artemis with Mount Tmolus (the citadel) in the background.
(*Author's photograph*)

Seleucid light cavalry clash with Roman *velites* skirmishers. (© *Graham Sumner*)

8. A Roman *equites* faces a Seleucid Companion. (© *Graham Sumner*)

Hard-pressed by a Roman legionary and fearing encirclement, a phalangite looks nervously over ┤ shoulder as the phalanx collapses around him. The long pikes of the phalanx were useless once ┤ir ranks were disrupted and the Roman swordsmen got to close quarters. (© *Graham Sumner*)

10. The heavily armoured cataphract cavalry of Antiochus III assaults the Roman left wing at Magnesia. (© *Graham Sumner*)

belonging to other generals he made the lives of his own very comfortable, spending prodigious amount on them and so encouraged the evils of both treachery and debauched living.

(Plut., *Sull*. 12.7–9)

Plutarch maintains that Sulla became rather obsessed with the idea of capturing Athens possibly from envy about its famous past or more probably spurred on in reaction to some of the abuse directed against him and his wife by Aristion from the city's walls. This Aristion comes in for some special criticism and indeed he behaved in such an archetypal tyrannical fashion that it is curious that the Athenians continued to follow him to the bitter end. And that end came towards the end of winter when famine had taken a terrible course with the inhabitants and when an assault was made on a stretch of wall near the Heptachalcum ('Place of the Seven Rosettes') which was reportedly left unguarded (Plut., *Sull*. 14.1). The soldiers were allowed to go berserk in their desire for slaughter and looting and thousands are said to have perished and that the blood of the killed ran from the Agora to the Ceramaicus just inside the Dipylon Gate. Sulla was finally prevailed upon by some Athenian exiles in his entourage and some of his fellow senators to halt this tragedy. Aristion, however, continued to hold out on the Acropolis and only surrendered when his supplies of water were exhausted.[15] The Piraeus held out for some days more and its capture was accompanied with indiscriminate burning.

It is surprising, seeing that Sulla had no fleet worth mentioning, that Mithridates did not order Archelaus to aid the Athenians in their struggle. And although Archelaus blockaded Attica with his ships, Plutarch states that he lent no material aid then or later.[16] On the other hand, Taxiles, another general of Mithridates, was marching down from Thrace with 100,000 infantry, 10,000 cavalry and 94 scythed chariots. Sulla moved his army out of Attica and into Boeotia to meet this new threat. Even when his force had been supplemented by a detachment led by L. Hortensius,[17] it was still incredibly outnumbered with barely 15,000 infantry and 1,500 cavalry, although it is noted that the superiority with the enemy lay in their cavalry numbers not in their infantry. Moreover, in Plutarch's account Taxiles appears to have been replaced by Archelaus by the time the Pontic army arrived in Boeotia, the former plays only a subordinate role later in the campaign.[18] Plutarch draws heavily on his personal knowledge of the area especially in and around Chaeronea, but also on Sulla's memoirs which make the writer's earlier comments about Sulla and Athens seem nonsensical when viewed together. Plutarch states that because of the disparity in numbers the Roman troops were understandably reluctant to fight.

It made the Romans afraid to venture out of their camp and Sulla found it impossible to force them to fight when they really wanted to

run away so had to sit tight and endure the enemy at close quarters
throwing insults ... but this actually brought him some advantages
since his opponents were lacking discipline and did not always obey
orders ... Now ... they became like a rabble ... and in the hope of
gains from looting they scattered far and wide ... They are said to
have destroyed the city of Panope and Lebadea ... Sulla was upset
and angry to observe that cities were being destroyed in front of him
but did not allow his men to remain idle.   (Plut., *Sull.* 16.3–5)

Sulla made his soldiers dig ditches and other tasks which the soldiers resented
as being beneath their status, and in the end they were goaded by these menial
tasks into demanding that they be allowed to fight the enemy.[19] A good
example of reverse psychology! But these comments do not synchronise at all
well with Plutarch's previous thoughts about the general pandering to his
troops and his compulsive desire to destroy Athens.

A great deal of manoeuvring went on before the two sides finally clashed.
The city of Chaeronea was threatened by Archelaus, and so a detachment
under A. Gabinius was sent which secured it for the Romans, although as
Plutarch says (*Sull.* 16.8) it was a close-run thing. Both armies were moving
around Boeotia looking for the best spot to allow good defence and a favourable
field of battle. Sulla also ordered an outflanking exercise when he found that
Archelaus had pitched camp in the neighbourhood of Mount Acontium and
Mount Hedylium and had occupied a 'cone-shaped hill' called Thurium
(Plut., *Sull.* 17.4). Two men from Chaeronea – Homoloichus and Anaxidamus
– notified Sulla about a little known path which, if followed by a troop of
soldiers, would bring then out above the enemy's current placement on
Thurium. From that vantage point they would be able to launch an attack and
drive the enemy down into the plain. Sulla found the plan agreeable and his
men set off at about the same time as the Romans drew up their line of battle.
The Romans had cavalry on each wing, the right commanded by Sulla the left
by his legate L. Licinius Murena. A reserve force under Ser. Sulpicius Galba
and Hortensius was stationed away from the main body in order that they
could be called upon to bridge any gaps which might open in the Roman ranks
and to especially avoid any outflanking by the enemy. It was quite obvious that
the enemy intended to try and employ its superiority in cavalry on its own
wings to engulf the Romans.

The men who had gone by the secret path – unknown to the Pontic invaders
that is – arrived as the main hostilities were beginning; and the intended effect
certainly worked in that those guarding Thurium were thrown into confusion
and were either killed by their assailants or rushed down in a panic to rejoin the
main body of the army so unsettling the main contingent.[20] Indeed, Sulla saw

the uncertainty among the enemy and set his infantry to advance rapidly, closing the gap between the two fronts so as to cause the use of the chariots to become ineffective. As Plutarch points out chariots need space to move around and accelerate to a speed when their scythed wheels can be put to good use. Where there is no space or time for either they are best left parked out of the way. However, Archelaus was also no second-rate commander and he followed his plan to use his right wing in an enveloping movement on the Roman left wing. Hortensius saw what was happening and responded by ordering his reserve troops to attack Archelaus' flank. The latter again, as if in an intricate chess match, wheeled his cavalry around to attack the attackers who were soon in trouble. Sulla was informed of the situation and raced from the right wing to the rescue, while Archelaus, one step ahead at this stage, intended going around behind and attacking the Roman right wing. At the same time Taxiles in charge of the enemy right wing led a brigade called the 'Bronze Shields' against Murena. Now Sulla was uncertain of which way to turn, but decided on the status quo returning to his own position and tackling Archelaus after first ordering Hortensius to bring up help to Murena. Sulla found his right wing holding out well and with his appearance it started to advance driving the enemy in front of the line against the Molus River. Sulla then went to check on Murena found this wing also victorious and joined the pursuit of the defeated.

As usual when the rout began serious casualties affected the side in retreat. Plutarch (*Sull.* 19.4) states that 90,000 of Archelaus' infantry were killed, with just 10,000 escaping to Chalcis on Euboea. The Roman losses were ludicrously light if Sulla's memoirs can be believed for Plutarch comments that the general found that only fourteen men were lost and that two of these turned up later. In Greek fashion, trophies were set up to celebrate this fine victory, one where Archelaus' men started to withdraw against Sulla, and another at Thurium, dedicated in particular to the men of Chaeronea who had given vital help in securing the triumph. A victory celebration was later held in Thebes, again very much in emulation of Greek practices, but the Thebans were not treated favourably by Sulla, possibly because of their history of Medizing or because of a current sympathy with Mithridates. In fact he removed half of Theban territory and rented it out so that the revenue from these lands would be used to repay the money which he had removed from Delphi.[21]

The war was certainly not over in Greece because a new army sent by Mithridates was soon on the scene led by Dorylaeus. This general had arrived by ship in Chalcis with 80,000 infantry and quickly occupied Boeotia as Sulla was marching into Thessaly and was keen to offer battle despite Archelaus' misgivings of such an offensive approach. Sulla turned south immediately and the two forces clashed near Mount Tilphossium at the southern end of Lake Copais near Orchomenus, where Dorylaeus came off the worse. Sulla now had the advantage of a successful battle behind him and Mithridatic generals who were no longer keen to engage him. However, Archelaus was happy with his encampment near Orchomenus which was suitable for an army with a strong cavalry element.[22] The two sides were quite close to one another and Sulla decided to dig ditches on either side of Archelaus' new camp in order to disrupt any cavalry manoeuvres. Obviously such a move was bound to bring on a strong response and the Romans were put to flight until:

> ... Sulla himself leaped down from his horse and seized a standard and pushed his way forward through those who were intent on running away, and as he went he shouted, 'Romans, I shall be able to die honourably, but as for you, when people inquire, where it was you betrayed your general remember to say "It was at Orchomenus."' And these words had the required effect.
>
> (Plut., *Sull.* 21.2)

The troops who were in flight came to their senses and turned around and followed Sulla; and extra troops then came up and turned a potential rout into a famous victory. The troops and labourers were rested then resumed their task. Again the enemy responded and in the next fight a son of Archelaus was killed, and the work of digging ditches continued.[23] Next day the Romans started their construction job again and the enemy again responded, but this time the situation turned into a full-scale battle in which the enemy seems – the details are obscure – to have been completely destroyed.

> The marshes were filled with their blood and the lakes with their bodies. Even today almost 200 years after this battle it is still possible to find in the mud bows and helmets of the invaders, swords and bits of their breastplates.   (Plut., *Sull.* 21.4)

Soon afterwards discussions were arranged through an intermediary from Delos, and these took place at Delium where Sulla, on behalf of Rome, and Archelaus, for the king, discussed possible terms. Sulla was keen to conclude the war to his satisfaction but was also aware that an army under L. Valerius Flaccus had been sent out to take over the campaign although at first the two commanders had cooperated. Sulla's official position was actually as a *hostis* or enemy of Rome, he and his political allies – which presumably included all his officers and the citizen legionaries – had lost their rights as Romans which included their lands and any other property. Confiscation of property and estate was the usual punishment for those exiled, while a possible capital punishment may have been extended in the event that any tried to return to Italy.[24] This was precisely Sulla's intention: to lead his army back to Italy march again on Rome and defeat his enemies led now by the consuls elected for

85, L. Cornelius Cinna (his third consulship) and Cn. Papirius Carbo. The conclusion of a peace treaty with Mithridates was thus complicated by domestic political issues and the Pontic king knew this.

Sulla's terms were: Mithridates must surrender his conquest of the Roman province of Asia, and Paphlagonia, return Bithynia to its king Nicomedes, and Cappadocia to its king Ariobarzanes, pay a war indemnity of 2,000 talents and turn over to the Romans a substantial part of his war fleet. The indemnity was a large one for so small a state but is perhaps related to Mithridates' known personal wealth. At first the king sought to make compromises such as retaining Paphlagonia and haggling over the number of ships he should relinquish perhaps hoping that Sulla's worries about the situation in Rome would make him a weaker negotiator. He was soon to be disillusioned. Sulla was marching north through Thrace towards the Hellespont aiming to take the war into Asia. His response to the king's attempt at intrigue was typically Roman:

> 'What! Mithridates thinks he has a right to Paphlagonia and refuses to give up his fleet? I think he should come and cringe at my feet if I was good enough to allow him to retain his right hand with which he has killed so many Romans! He will soon change his mind the moment I cross into Asia!' (Plut., *Sull.* 23.3)

The king's envoys were suitably impressed. Archelaus who had remained with Sulla during these talks now returned to Mithridates with the ultimatum. He soon returned with full compliance, but a request that the king of Pontus had a personal meeting with Sulla. It is said (Plut., *Sull.* 23.6) that the army of Flaccus now commanded by C. Flavius Fimbria, who had connived at his commander's murder, was already active in Asia Minor, and Mithridates wanted to prevent any further defeats. The king came to Sulla at Dardanus in the Troad in 85, and although he started to justify his actions he clearly saw that, under the circumstances, he had no option than to accept the terms as offered. Mithridates was then welcomed as 'Friend and Ally' of Rome and departed again for Pontus. The Roman side to this agreement as a whole was not happy with the arrangements with a ruler responsible for such outrageous behaviour against their people. However, a new civil war was looming in Italy so there was hardly any choice in the matter. A chapter may have been concluded but hardly the full story.

Chapter 7

The Adventure of Murena

Up the airy mountain,
Down the rushy glen,
We daren't go a-hunting,
For fear of little men.
(W. Allingham)

What little we know of the ability of Lucius Licinius Murena comes from the biased evidence of a defence speech given by Cicero in 63 BC on behalf of Murena's son who was his client accused of electoral corruption in the consular elections for 62 which he had recently won. He was acquitted of all charges brought against him.

> ... if you consider carefully what Mithridates could have done, what he actually did and what sort of man he was, you will certainly place this king above all others with whom the Roman people have waged war. This man Lucius Sulla, a pugnacious, bold and no mean commander, with the greatest and bravest army ... let go in peace even though he had brought war to the whole of Asia. This man Lucius Murena, father of my client, left defeated but not crushed having attacked him with great force and vigilance.
>
> (Cic., *Pro Mur.* 32)

Cicero was, of course, under the circumstances of his client's trial for electoral corruption, being extremely economical with the truth. Sulla's decision to grant Mithridates very reasonable terms in 85 were – and the protagonists knew it – governed by events occurring in Italy and in Rome, and especially Sulla's determination to return home to restore his political position and his name. Mithridates got off virtually scot-free, because Sulla wanted to re-embark the majority of the forces at his disposal for a new campaign against his political opponents in Italy. His legate Murena was left in charge of the province of Asia, while his general marched north from the Troad to deal with Gaius Flavius Fimbria who had been campaigning in Bithynia and was then camped near Thyateira (Plut., *Sull.* 25.1).[1] Fimbria's murder of his commanding officer the consul Lucius Valerius Flaccus some months before does not appear to have endeared him to his troops. As Sulla's army approached and began to construct its own camp, Fimbria's men began to openly desert in large numbers, and welcomed their compatriots. Fimbria's future looked highly uncertain, and he pre-empted capture and possible execution by committing suicide.[2] Sulla sailed from Ephesus soon after this union of Roman armies.

However, a large fine had been imposed on the cities of Asia by Sulla, in his view, for their betrayal of the Roman resident communities which had been massacred in 89. The Asia Minor cities, not just within the Roman province, but throughout the region were forced into making tough choices between the various key players, often with no chance of emerging without physical or fiscal damage. Indeed the 80s began a period lasting almost a century when many of the ancient cities of Asia Minor were drained of their wealth by the Romans, often by different factions among the governing elite.[3] Sulla saw no reason why these cities should not foot the entire bill for the war. He had after all come to their 'aid' when they had been 'conquered' by Mithridates. Sulla is said to have been particularly vengeful against the Ephesians on account of their duplicity, first favouring the Romans and then turning against them (App., *Mith.* 9.61). The other cities were obliged to send their chief men to Sulla who was then in Ephesus and these, according to Appian but probably from Sulla himself via Livy's history, were castigated by him.

> 'We first came to Asia with an army when the king of Syria, Antiochus (III) was devastating your lands. We defeated him and fixed the frontiers of his kingdom beyond the River Halys and the Taurus Mountains. We did not occupy your lands when you had in fact become our subjects, instead we freed you except for a few places which were given to Eumenes and the Rhodians, our allies in that war not as dependent states but as our clients. When the Lycians complained to us about the Rhodians we freed them too and this is proof of the status of Rhodes. This was the way we behaved towards you. However, when Attalus (III) Philometor bequeathed his kingdom to us you gave aid to Aristonicus against us for four years until he was captured when most of you compelled by need and fear returned to your former allegiance. Notwithstanding, after twenty-four years in which you became wealthy and displayed both private and public munificence, you again became arrogant through peace and luxury and took the opportunity while we were occupied in Italy either to join in alliance with Mithridates or joined him when he invaded. Most outrageous of all you obeyed his order to kill all the Italians in your cities including women and children ... it is necessary ... some punishment should be imposed on you altogether

for these crimes ... However, may the Romans never be accused of indiscriminate killings, random confiscations, encouraging slave revolts or other barbaric actions. From a desire to spare even now the Greek name and reputation which is so famous throughout Asia and for the sake of that reputation which is still revered by the Romans ...'   (App., *Mith.* 9.62)

Imposed on the Greek cities was a fine equivalent of five years annual tribute to be paid immediately plus the cost of the war, a sum to be determined by Sulla himself, who sent officials to collect the money.[4] The cities of Asia Minor were made penniless overnight and many had to borrow heavily at exorbitant interest rates from private individuals or from Italian and Roman merchants to fulfil these demands. If they failed to pay on time the threat was implicit: total destruction of the city by violence.

Because of Sulla's decision, partly caused by his own financial needs, the coastal cities were no longer in a position to defend themselves from pirates who proliferated having been encouraged in their activities by Mithridates. The problem had become so acute that cities such as Iassos in the Troad and Clazomenae in Ionia had been captured and plundered as had the main urban centres on the islands of Samos and Samothrace in the east and northern Aegean respectively. The extent of their power can be gauged by the fact that they were operating out of numerous bases in western Cilicia close to Rhodes and other major Asia Minor cities. Even with the fleet that Sulla certainly possessed by the end of the war, he chose not to involve himself in a conflict with the pirate bands, possibly seeing the campaign as a long and difficult one, remembering his own experience as proconsul there, or more probably wanting to return to Italy as rapidly as he could. It was probably suggested by later writers that he left the pirate menace as a festering wound as an additional punishment for the region now caught between unpredictable seaborne attacks and Roman indifference.[5]

Murena was left in charge of the province of Asia retaining the two legions which had previously been under the command of Flavius Fimbria. His status was quite illegal having been appointed governor by a renegade general, although he appears to have possessed the rank of praetor and hence ordinarily would have qualified for such a position.[6] However, by the end of 85 the Roman Empire was again in a state of civil war; and it perhaps accounts for Murena's determination to obtain a triumph.[7] Although the region was technically at peace, and certainly exhausted by the previous war, Murena cast around for an excuse to revive the war with Pontus. He soon found these! Mithridates may have been defeated but it was not in his nature to be idle for long. He seems to have immediately taken issue with the Colchians and the tribes of the Cimmerian Bosporus for rebelling against him (App., *Mith.* 9.64). The former obtained peace by requesting a son of Mithridates be installed as their king although that situation was of short duration.[8] Mithridates levied an army and had built a large fleet to attack the tribes of what is now the Crimea, but there were fears that this rearming would be directed against the Romans. Archelaus, Mithridates' senior general in the last war, had fallen from grace and fled to Murena and urged proactive measures. Murena needed no further encouragement and feeling that he had some justification in that Mithridates had not returned the whole of Cappadocia to Ariobarzanes, as he had promised Sulla in their treaty, led his forces out of Asia *provincia* through Cappadocia and into Pontus.

Heading along the coast of the Euxine, Murena attacked the town of Comana Pontica (App., *Mith.* 9.64) and sacked a temple complex and in some encounter killed some cavalry. The town is not said to have fallen to Murena and the temple may well have been situated outside the urban area. Mithridates sent envoys to demand the Romans cease from breaking their recent agreement, a treaty which Murena, like the king, could ignore since there had yet to be official ratification by the senate. Having obtained some plunder Murena wintered his forces in Cappadocia. Mithridates sent an embassy to Rome and to Sulla to repeat his objections to Murena's attacks. But in the meantime with the advent of spring Murena crossed the Halys River into Pontus and began a systematic plundering of villages and towns which offered no defence as the king waited for a response from Italy. At the end of this campaign, towards the end of summer 82, Murena went into Phrygia and Galatia 'loaded with plunder' (App., *Mith.* 9.65).[9] Mithridates must have known, like Murena, that there was fierce fighting taking place in Italy between pro- and anti-Sullan forces and an incredibly weakened senate, both in terms of numbers and authority, caught between the two. Any response to the 'Pontic Question' could easily be tossed aside by either side on the grounds that there was no one to enforce a directive. And no one could be sure that any response would or could arrive in Asia Minor. Still, perhaps against the odds a senator named as Calidius did indeed arrive from Rome. Appian says that he was a representative of the senate (*Mith.* 9.65) but that he carried no formal direction or decree to Mithridates' complaint. Quite clearly, if this senator arrived some time during 82 the senate was in no position to offer much guidance; and, indeed, while Calidius in public stressed that the king's position should be respected, in private talks with Murena he probably also underlined the fact that if the general wanted the laurels of a military success there was little the senate could do to prevent it.[10]

After Calidius' departure, Murena made no radical changes to the plans of the campaign, and so the king now responded by ordering Gordius, one of his own generals, to make retaliatory attacks into the Roman province. Gordius apparently accomplished just this, taking a fair measure of plunder of materials and humans, and then came face to face with Murena's forces with only a river between them. A full-scale engagement did not begin however until Mithridates himself appeared with additional troops and the Pontic army launched itself across the river. Murena held them initially but then fell back to a defensive position on a hill nearby. There the Roman troops withstood an onslaught probably until sunset when the enemy forces withdrew. Appian states that Roman losses were heavy and were made heavier still in the retreat which lay through rough mountainous ground back into Phrygia pursued for some of the time by Mithridates' forces.[11] Roman garrisons in Cappadocia were either overwhelmed or ejected, and it was remembered that Mithridates made elaborate sacrifices to Zeus Stratius or 'Zeus of the Armies,' in thanks for his great victory over the Romans.

Murena might have been expected to respond in turn once he had re-organized his forces. That did not happen however for news of this defeat had gone quickly to Rome where Sulla was now firmly in control as 'dictator for the reconstitution of the state'.[12] He sent as his representative Aulus Gabinius with instructions that Murena was to re-establish peaceful conditions and that reconciliation between Mithridates and Ariobarzanes of Cappadocia should be accomplished. Mithridates, ever the cunning diplomat, proposed that his daughter aged four be betrothed to the Cappadocian king and that in return he would retain not only that part of Cappadocia he already held but another section was to be added as well. This surprising arrangement was agreed, probably by Gabinius – Murena's role as senior Roman officer in Asia Minor seems to have been usurped by Sulla's envoy.[13] A banquet and games were held in celebration of the peace, and Appian concludes:

> Thus the second war between Mithridates and the Romans lasting
> about three years came to an end.   (App., *Mith.* 9.66)

Nothing more is heard of Murena's great adventure, which was really a very clumsy attempt to win military glory and which backfired heavily, although he seems to have celebrated a triumph on his return. His subsequent career seems to have stalled, nonetheless, and he may well have died soon after 81. He was certainly not alive when his son became consul in 62, a position he had aspired to but had not been able to achieve. The peace treaty was never ratified by the senate, but it still allowed Mithridates more power than he had before and, in theory at least, also left him to pose as an ally of the Romans, with quite considerable freedom to do as he chose just as long as he did not interfere with the province of Asia.[14] Moreover, Rome's willingness to make a peace at this juncture sent out a particularly telling message that could easily have been interpreted as a sign of weakness. True, Rome was now just starting a recovery from a decade of violent internecine strife and a new war in the east would not have been welcome. It would have been quite feasible financially since the Romans always had vast resources in terms of manpower and wealth compared to other ancient states, as events showed within a short time. But the pause also allowed Mithridates the opportunity to capitalize on this position. And he evidently wasted no time. Sulla's retirement in 79 followed by his death a year later also caused a lack of political continuity. His death was followed by an attempted coup by M. Aemilius Lepidus one of the consuls of 78 and this caused further uncertainty in Italy. For Mithridates VI Eupator the future looked very bright indeed!

Chapter 8

The Third Mithridatic War

Two generals were sent against Mithridates from Rome,
the first was the same Lucullus who had served as prefect
of the fleet under Sulla, and the second was Pompey, by whom
the whole of the king's lands and the lands next to these up
to the River Euphrates, on account of ... and desire for ...
which the war with Mithridates supplied, were brought into the
Roman Empire.   (App., *Mith*. 10.68)

The apparent soft approach by the Roman government – was Sulla dis-
interested in the fate of Asia, he had been governor of Cilicia in the 90s, or was
he taken in by Mithridates?[1] Whatever the reason Mithridates was let off the
hook and he knew it. Within a year he was carrying on his war against the tribes
of the Crimea and was able to impose on them one of his sons, Machares, as
their king. He was not as lucky against the Greeks of the eastern Euxine, probably Trapezus, where he came off worse in fighting. He also busied himself
with embassies to Rome to clarify his terms, but these no doubt had to contend
with envoys from Ariobarzanes complaining that Pontus still occupied the
greater part of Cappadocia. Sulla sent orders to Mithridates demanding
immediate withdrawal. The Pontic presence was pulled back, but Mithridates
was a cunning fox who certainly fully understood the phrase '*carpe diem*' even if
he did not speak the language, also sent a new legation to Rome for further
talks. This arrived after Sulla's death when the senate was facing a series of
new crises in Italy and the question of Pontus was delayed. In the absence of
any firm direction emanating from Rome Mithridates seized his chance
and persuaded another son-in-law Tigranes, the king of Armenia, to invade
Cappadocia.

This event, as related by Appian (*Mith*. 10.67), is a rather strange episode
dismissed in a single sentence but if true caused incredible upheaval and the
forced removals of people on such a scale not seen since the Persian Wars of
the fifth century. Tigranes is said to have thrown a cordon around the entire
kingdom and rounded up no less than 300,000 people whom he led off to
populate his new city named after the king himself, Tigranocerta.[2] The ruse
did not fool the Romans although no movement was made by the governor of

Asia to intervene on the side of the Cappadocian monarch who was also supposedly an ally of Rome. Ariobarzanes must have despaired of the value of Roman friendship while Mithridates can only have regarded his tactics as worthwhile and extremely lucrative.

The Roman proconsul of Asia *provincia* was stymied in his possible courses of action because of the new crisis unfolding in Italy at precisely this moment. Lepidus' rebellion had been a serious attack on the heart of the empire that it fizzled out was due to the firm handling of the government by the consuls of 77 and the military accomplishments of Q. Lutatius Catulus, Lepidus' consular colleague, who utilized the services of Pompey.[3] Lepidus was forced to evacuate Italy for Sardinia where he died of illness, but only after fierce fighting had taken place on the island. The crisis ought to have solved itself, but unfortunately M. Perperna, the commander of Lepidus' forces now ferried his troops north to the coast of Provence, where he is said to have picked up other survivors of Lepidus' uprising, and plundered the countryside, probably for supplies.[4] He did not remain here for long and shortly afterwards joined the governor of Hispania Citerior,[5] Q. Sertorius, who was also in open rebellion against the Roman government.

Sertorius is a fascinating figure who deserves some comment. A former junior officer of Marius in the wars against the Cimbri and Teutones, since then he had risen in the ranks of the senate to become a praetor maintaining his loyalty to his former chief and consistently hostile to Sulla in the 80s. When Sulla returned from the East in 83 he was already in Spain. After Sulla's victory and election as dictator at the end of 82 he denounced the new regime formed a new senate from among his followers, and then repulsed any attempts by the administration at Rome to take back the province over which he ruled as representing what he regarded as the legitimate government. The arrival of Perperna enhanced his position and brought an opportunity to put further pressure on Rome. That that pressure should involve diplomatic overtures across the entire length of the Mediterranean says something of the genius of Sertorius.

In a remarkable show of 'one-upmanship' Sertorius despatched two of his subordinates, Lucius Fannius and Lucius Magius, as envoys to Mithridates suggesting an alliance.[6] The king is said to have found the proposal attractive although what he hoped to gain from this act is not at all clear beyond what was obviously a propaganda coup for the participants in the deal.

> Mithridates concurred with the offer and sent a legation to Sertorius who presented these to his senate and took great pride in the fact that his reputation extended to Pontus and that he could now lay siege to Rome from both east and west. He made a treaty with Mithridates

giving him Asia, Bithynia, Paphlagonia, Cappadocia and Galatia and
sent Marcus Varius to the king as general and Magius and Fannius as
advisors.   (App., *Mith.* 10.68)[7]

Sertorius may have believed that with a pact between the two known at Rome
some pressure against him in Spain would be relieved. In that hope however he
was to be deceived since the Romans had already responded in 77 by ordering
Pompey to proceed to Spain with an army to augment the forces of the
proconsul of Hispania Ulterior Q. Caecilius Metellus Pius. Against Mithridates the Romans assigned the consul L. Licinius Lucullus the command of a
new war in the East at the beginning of 74.[8]

It shows something of, on the one hand, the extent of Mithridates' ambitions
and, on the other, the extreme pressures on the Roman government. Mithridates, who had now evidently regained much of this military strength as a
result of five years of peaceful conditions, made elaborate preparations. It is
stated explicitly by Plutarch (*Luc.* 7.4) that he chose not to rely on native levies
as in the past, but equipped and trained his troops according to Roman
practices. It is also claimed that he had access to huge manpower resources.
Intent on another invasion of Roman territory, Appian claims that Mithridates
collected a fighting force of 140,000 infantry and 16,000 cavalry (*Mith.* 10.69),
which he ordered first against Paphlagonia and then Bithynia at the start of 74.[9]
The Roman response may indeed have been proactive in that both consuls were
assigned this war zone and may have already been earmarked for this job in 75
at their election. If so it suggests that the senate was aware of the build-up in
Pontic power and the inevitability of further hostilities in this region. Yet
Lucullus was allowed to levy just one legion, which he supplemented with
the two legions already stationed in Asia, those formerly of Flavius Fimbria.
His total forces were probably no more than 20,000 infantry and cavalry.[10]
Lucullus was obviously based either in Pergamum or Ephesus while
M. Aurelius Cotta, his consular colleague, seems to have chosen Chalcedon
as a base rather than Nicomedia or Nicaea. It is possible that Cotta arrived after
Mithridates had already occupied much of Bithynia.

The king of Pontus was clearly well informed about the placement of the
Roman forces, with the newly acquired Bithynian province identified as a
much softer target than the province of Asia. Mithridates seems to have swept
down from Pontus onto the coast of the Propontis (Sea of Marmara) and Cotta,
with perhaps only local militia to add to his own troops seemingly numbering
no more than two or three cohorts, was rapidly cornered. His prefect of the
fleet, a certain Rutilius Nudus, came close to disaster by offering battle to the
Pontic army where his forces suffered major casualties outside the walls of
the city.[11] Quite why the Roman forces should have been focussed in Asia

leaving Bithynia vulnerable predictably receives no comment from ancient sources. A high degree of lacklustre planning and coordination does seem evident with hindsight, nevertheless. Even if, as Plutarch says (*Luc.* 7.5–6), Lucullus was busy attending to provincial administration or rather mal-administration especially on the question of taxation, Mithridates' movements could surely have been monitored, since an army of more than 100,000 with its attendant hordes of camp followers should have been easily covered. That it was not simply shows again that the Romans were hardly as efficient in their military expertise as is sometimes assumed. From near disaster, once again the Romans were on the back foot and had to retrieve the situation and counter-attack.

Cotta was besieged at Chalcedon and Lucullus moved north to come to his aid, and though the details provided by our sources are quite incomprehensible here, Mithridates appears to have quit his siege of Chalcedon and turned his attention to Cyzicus. Yet, the forces of Pontus had made a successful attack on the harbour of Chalcedon and the Roman fleet had been captured (App., *Mith.*, 10.71), and relief from Lucullus did not appear imminent.[12] We are not told why the king should leave Chalcedon alone when he was clearly in a superior position there. It is of course conceivable that Mithridates felt vulnerable in that part of the Bosporus with Byzantium behind him and Roman land forces in Thrace so somehow contrived to spirit (it was 'a dark and rainy night' says Plutarch, *Luc.* 9.1) his troops across the Sea of Marmara – possibly using captured Roman ships – and into the face of Lucullus' advance and arrived at Cyzicus (modern Bandirma). It may also be that Mithridates' main armament had not been brought into use for the attack on Chalcedon, for at Cyzicus Appian contends that he had an army of 300,000 (App., *Mith.* 11.72), and that he simply lacked the siege equipment to carry a successful campaign further north. His forces outside Cyzicus certainly appear to have been much more substantial than those he commanded further north. Cotta got off lightly, but significantly his command was not renewed. Meanwhile, Lucullus had encountered enemy forces in Phrygia as he moved north, and there seems to have been some inconclusive fighting (Plut., *Luc.* 8.5–7), before the Romans also arrived near Cyzicus.

The siege of Cyzicus has elaborate coverage in both the accounts of Appian and Plutarch; and the events themselves clearly left an impression on ancient writers. It seems to have been one of the more famous of ancient sieges. However, it has to be said that some of the details are siege *topoi* or the usual elements included in any description of a besieged city in antiquity. Many of these are similar if not pointedly derived from descriptions of sieges such as that of Tyre by Alexander the Great (331) and of Syracuse by the Romans led by M. Claudius Marcellus (214–212).[13] Cyzicus, like Tyre, was a city situated on an island just off the mainland, and like Tyre and Syracuse, possessed a good harbour.[14] Still, unlike most ancient cities under siege, but in emulation of recent events at Chalcedon, Cyzicus refused to bow to the oppressor. No fifth columnist opened a gate there and among the inhabitants there seems to have been a unity of purpose, which finally won the day. It is also clear that Lucullus' presence with his army encamped within view of the city walls also bolstered the resolve of the Cyziceans in turning back the attackers.

Lucullus clearly arrived in the area after the king and camped not far away. Mithridates had taken up the usual encircling position, in ten camps according to Plutarch (*Luc.* 9.3) on the landward side of the city. Lucullus' army was initially probably to the south, but then he moved his camp further inland to prevent supplies reaching his enemy from the interior. He established a new camp on a prominent hill still within sight of the city but at the rear of the besiegers so that they too became besieged.[15] Mithridates was apparently kept ignorant of the increasingly desperate situation with his army but, at the same time, seems to have realised that in order to break out he had to take the city.[16]

So notwithstanding the zeal of the defenders and the difficulties imposed on the Pontic army by the Romans, the besiegers employed all sorts of novel techniques and siege engines. Appian says that a double wall or mole was constructed to block the entrance of the harbour, while Plutarch more realistically notes a naval blockade of the island. And a trench was constructed which circumvallated the walls (App., *Mith.* 11.73), though that cannot be correct unless a sector of the city was actually on the mainland. Mounds were raised on which catapults could be employed against the walls. A ramp was supposedly built extending from nearby Mount Dindymus. Towers of various sorts were built, some to contain battering rams, others to allow access on to the walls. One with a height of 100 cubits, roughly 30 metres, was built, on which another tower was constructed which contained a ballista for hurling projectiles such as bolts and stones. Two quinqueremes, the largest warships available, were lashed together so that another tower could be raised on their combined upper decks and this monster was towed against the wall on the seaward side of the city. The intention was to extend a bridge from this tower enabling troops on board to cross into the city. Just before the action began 3,000 Cyzicean prisoners were sent towards the walls in the hope that they could persuade their fellow townspeople to save them by opening the gates and surrendering the city, but the defenders stood firm. The fate of the prisoners is not related (App., *Mith.* 11.73), but Plutarch says (*Luc.* 9.1) that 3,000 Cyziceans were lost in action in the battle at Chalcedon; these were probably the unfortunate captives.

After this the various war machines were advanced. The bridge from the tower on the warships was projected to the walls and, although it surprised the defenders, just four enemy soldiers are said to have gained the wall before countermeasures such as pouring burning pitch down onto it forced a with-drawal of the enemy. Plutarch also notes that the defenders took heart from the fact that a gale caused a number of the siege engines and towers to collapse (*Luc.* 10.2; cf. App., *Mith.* 11.74), while at other times sustained assaults on the walls from the mainland were met with various ingenious responses: lopping off the beaks of battering rams, using baskets of wool to deaden the effect of battering rams, using water and vinegar to extinguish burning missiles launched from catapults or ballistas:

> In short they tried everything that was within human capacity to achieve, and although they toiled to the extremes of perseverance a part of the wall was still weakened sufficiently by fire to collapse one evening, but because of the heat the enemy did not venture in. That night the Cyziceans constructed another wall next to it.
>
> (App., *Mith.* 11.74)

Mithridates clearly had not expected such a fierce defence of the city and eventually having become aware of the plight of his army he decided to send his cavalry and baggage train inland. This appears to have occurred at the end of the campaigning season with the onset of the winter, probably about November 74. Lucullus caught up with these despite worsening weather conditions – Plutarch describes 'falling snow' (*Luc.* 11.2) – in which his forces sustained casualties. An engagement took place near a town described as Apollonia, and the captured materials and pack animals were brought back to the Roman camp.[17] This reverse certainly shook the king's resolve and he now planned a withdrawal but in good order (Plut., *Luc.* 11.5).

Appian and Plutarch again diverge in their accounts of Mithridates' retreat. For Appian the rising levels of distress among his forces caused by the usual diseases associated with overcrowding, lack of hygiene and meagre provisions, which had led to cases of cannibalism, caused the king to make his escape by ship. It is interesting to note that the Pontic forces still controlled the sea and that Lucullus had not taken any steps to introduce a Roman fleet into the area. Mithridates therefore always had this avenue of retreat although the main bulk of his army could probably not be easily ferried out of Cyzicus. Two strands of this episode are immediately apparent.

Plutarch (*Luc.* 11.5) writes that Mithridates planned to send out a diver-sionary attack by sea led by a certain Aristonicus, but that this commander was betrayed to the Romans virtually before he had set out. With him was captured a huge sum of money which was intended for the subversion of Roman soldiers. Aristonicus was supposed to head into the 'Greek Sea' – presumably the Aegean – and move south deep within the Roman-held territory. Quite what this Pontic general was meant to accomplish is left unclear, but there may be connection here with the ill-disciplined legions Lucullus had inherited from Murena, which had originally been commanded by Fimbria. Yet Plutarch has already noted (*Luc* 7.1) a restoration in discipline in precisely those legions. Perhaps the new regimen was resented and only skin-deep. However, there are further problems with this scenario. It implies that Lucullus had split his forces which seems unlikely from the accounts of the siege, and would surely have been unwise if there were lingering doubts about the loyalty of some of his troops. So if it was not these who were the intended targets of Mithridates' intrigues and bribery then it can only refer to the individual garrisons in the towns of the Troad and further south in the eastern Aegean region.

When Mithridates heard that his latest stratagem had been foiled he fled by sea leaving his generals to extricate his army if they could. Plutarch suggests that an utter catastrophe overtook the invaders soon after this with losses placed at 300,000, in other words the entire Pontic army, with 20,000 killed at the River Granicus caught in their retreat by the Romans. This retreat to the west of Cyzicus is also puzzling seeing that the way home to Pontus was in the opposite direction. This may indicate that the Roman control of the interior beyond Cyzicus meant that no escape could be accomplished in that direction. While the argument for an impassable Roman cordon is attractive, it does leave the objective of the Pontic army very unclear unless it was aiming to reach a safe harbour town which could then have been used as a way of leaving the area by sea. A sort of 'Dunkirk' exercise may have been envisaged. To further compound the problem, it is also possible that Plutarch's knowledge of the geography of Asia Minor was simply at fault and he was not aware, or cared, that he was being inaccurate.

Lucullus entered Cyzicus in triumph then moved to the Hellespont where a fleet remarkably it seems was rather belatedly built and equipped.[18] While he was in the Troad, a small Pontic squadron of thirteen warships was sighted heading for Lemnos. Lucullus who had an excellent record as a naval commander at once launched his own ships to intercept the enemy.[19] This move proved to be a success and the enemy commander Isidorus was killed (Plut., *Luc*. 12.2) and the Romans then went on to search for other Pontic warships with which the unlucky Isidorus had hoped to rendezvous. These were eventually discovered close to the shore, perhaps at Lemnos, although this is not specified by Plutarch, and when they saw the Romans approaching in customary fashion they drew up their ships onto the beach and repelled any attempt at landing by those on the sea. Lucullus then landed troops on the island who managed to attack those on the shore by their ships from the rear. This caused a rout to begin, hand-to-hand combat among the ships, some of which were launched in an attempt to escape. But there was none and the

Romans inflicted heavy casualties and captured numerous prisoners. Among these was a Roman named Marius who had served with Sertorius in Spain. His end Plutarch maintains was not a pleasant one!

> Many of the enemy were killed, naturally enough, and among those captured was Marius, the general sent by Sertorius. He had just one eye, and the troops had been under strict orders from Lucullus as soon as they set out not to kill any one-eyed man.[20] Lucullus wanted Marius to die under the most shameful insults.
>
> (Plut., *Luc.* 12.5)

Appian's account of the same episode is somewhat different. After the capture of Mithridates' cavalry and baggage train, he gives a quite detailed report of military events in Phrygia where at least one general of Mithridates – Eumachus – was active and clearly intent on drawing Roman manpower away from Cyzicus. He apparently drove deep into the south-east as far as Cilicia before being driven back by Deiotarus, tetrarch or ruler of Galatia. Plutarch was of course concerned with a biographical study of Lucullus, but his concentration on a single subject distorts by simplification what was a complex theatre of war. Appian in fact illustrates that the entire subcontinent was once again badly affected and in turmoil. He notes that, with the onset of winter, Mithridates' army starved because supplies could not be brought in by sea (*Mith.* 11.76), and that disease also took its toll and that when the Cyzicaeans showed no slackening in their determination to withstand any offensive against them, the king began to entertain the idea of abandoning the siege. And he went under cover of darkness with a fleet to Parium further west along the coast, and ordered his army to retreat further west to Lampsacus, at the entrance of the Hellespont. The soldiers suffered badly in this retreat with severe losses, says Appian, crossing the swollen river Aesepus where they were attacked by the Romans. Still, a large number must have made it to Lampsacus since these were besieged by Lucullus but were rescued by ships sent by Mithridates. A garrison was left in Lampsacus commanded jointly by a Roman named Varius, a Paphlagonian named Alexander and a eunuch called Dionysius. Mithridates took off with the bulk of his army and fleet to Nicomedia but large-scale damage with much loss of life occurred on the way because of stormy conditions.[21] The option of a withdrawal by land from Cyzicus was therefore not a viable alternative for the king and indeed he was lucky to extract survivors from his army and bring them home.

Lucullus is said now to have collected a fleet drawn from the province of Asia (App., *Mith.* 11.77). This he divided among himself and a number of other commanders. One of these, Valerius Triarius, set out up the coast of the Propontis to the city of Apamea which he took, and where the Romans appear to have butchered most of the population. Another naval commander, Barba attacked and took Prusias (modern Bursa) and from there Nicaea which had been vacated by its Pontic garrison. Appian's account throws considerable light on the complexities of the situation within Bithynia, which plainly shows the extent to which Mithridates had controlled the eastern end of the Propontis, how crucial the siege of Cyzicus was to his future plans, and how important a victory it was for the Romans. Once Mithridates abandoned his attempt to take Cyzicus his position was immeasurably weaker than it had been before.

Lucullus in the meantime is reported to have captured thirteen enemy ships at the 'Harbour of the Achaeans,' close to Ilium in the Troad, and went in pursuit of the remnants of the Pontic garrison which had retreated from Lampsacus.[22] These had not followed their king east to Nicomedia but had evidently sailed south, perhaps at Mithridates' orders to stir up trouble behind the Roman forces.[23] Lucullus caught up with this squadron which had anchored at a barren island near Lemnos, the battle which took place follows much the same order as the one recounted by Plutarch, but the denouement is quite at odds with that of the biographer.[24] The joint commanders of the Pontic forces, Varius, Alexander and Dionysius were found having taken refuge in a cave. Dionysius took poison and committed suicide, the other two were taken prisoner. Varius was immediately executed because Lucullus deemed it unsuitable that any Roman, even a rebel, should be kept as a prize to be displayed at his triumph on his return to Rome. Alexander, however, was placed under guard for expressly this purpose.

> He then sent letters wreathed with laurel to Rome, as is customary
> for those victorious in war, and then advanced into Bithynia.
>
> (App., *Mith.* 11.77)

Appian next reports more adverse weather conditions which affected the retreat of Mithridates into Pontus. It appears that he had left Nicomedia by ship but had been caught by a further storm probably while sailing along the south coast of the Euxine. Since Chalcedon was in Roman hands he probably went overland north from Nicomedia and then joined his warships, but it was a foolhardy exercise to undertake in the middle of winter. Yet the circumstances may have been forced on him by the Roman advance. He is said to have lost another 10,000 troops and sixty ships, his own ship was affected and he made for the shore in a small boat manned by pirates, and although warned by his friends of the risks involved, he came safely into Sinope (App., *Mith.* 11.78). From here he travelled to Amisus and started to organise the defence of his realm.

Mithridates sent messages calling for immediate aid to his son Machares, king over the peoples of the Cimmerian Bosphorus (eastern Crimea), and to

Tigranes, his son-in-law, king of Armenia. A member of the king's inner circle, a certain Diocles, was entrusted with gold and valuable gifts to attempt to win over neighbouring Scythian tribes, but this man at once deserted to the Romans taking the treasures with him. In spring 72 Lucullus invaded Pontus via Bithynia and Galatia (Plut., *Luc.* 14.1). Pontus is described as a wealthy land and to that point untouched by previous warfare (App., *Mith.* 11.78) although Murena had perhaps passed through roughly a decade before. The land, its people and its towns and villages were at least relatively unscathed in comparison to the more Hellenized areas further west. Because of Mithridates' recent reversal, there was no immediate opposition and so Lucullus plundered at will. Consequently, it is claimed that the bottom fell out of the slave market, while other foodstuffs remained unsold because of this glut of supplies which far outstripped demand (Plut., *Luc.* 14.1: 'There was no sale of anything to anybody because everyone had so much in abundance.'). The Romans besieged Amisus (Samsun), Eupatoria, and Themiscyra (Terme) and although ingenious siege techniques were employed by the invaders the inhabitants of each city successfully withstood these attacks.[25] They were also supported by their king who managed to maintain supplies of food, armour and reinforcements to the garrisons of these centres of resistance while at the same time recruiting a new army of 40,000 infantry and 4,000 cavalry. Unfortunately Appian provides no information about how the Pontic king was able to bypass the Roman forces encamped outside his cities, but Plutarch was clearly under the impression that Lucullus did not press home any attacks in this campaigning season and that his troops were disgruntled about his more peaceful methods of winning over these centres and that they were being deprived of plunder, especially when any effort to take Amisus was abandoned. This narrative does seem to contradict earlier tales of extensive looting and it may be that both ancient sources were short of material here, the one inventing suitable anecdotes about sieges while the other wrote about the start of unrest in Lucullus' army, which was indeed to become a problem later on, in order to pad out in their works a part of the campaign in which exciting details were few and far between.

In the spring of 71 Lucullus led his forces away from the coastal belt of Pontus and into the mountains in search of his quarry. Mithridates, who had spent the winter at the town of Cabira levying and training his new army, had wisely posted scouts to warn him of the Romans' progress. In command of these he had placed Phoenix, a member of the royal family. When Lucullus was first sighted Phoenix, honouring the terms of his appointment, sent messages to his king and then deserted to the Romans with all his troops. Lucullus emerged from the mountains where his cavalry appears to have come off the worse for wear in an engagement with the Pontic cavalry. The Roman legions were clearly either not in a position to be deployed or perhaps were some way behind the cavalry units of the army, which may have been sent ahead in a reconnaissance exercise. It is also possible, but not stated, that the horsemen involved in this reverse were levies drawn not from Italy but from more local areas and lacked good training. To come off worse now against Mithridates, who was immeasurably weaker than he had been at Cyzicus does strike as being a little strange if not contrived by the ancient writers. Indeed Lucullus is given a speech by Plutarch (*Luc.* 14.4–6) in which he answered complaints that he was delaying his campaign by staying close to a series of safe havens when he should have been pursuing Mithridates. Lucullus is supposed to have countered this by declaring that he wanted Mithridates to become powerful again so that he could be defeated in Pontus and not given the opportunity to flee either into the wilds of the Caucasus or to his relative the king of Armenia. Both possible events it was argued could result in drawing the Romans into new and unlooked for wars. The theme appears to be that of *hubris* or overweening pride, a label Lucullus later had difficulty throwing off, and as events immediately proved his pride was at once humbled by Mithridates' defeat of the Roman cavalry near Cabira.

Lucullus seems to have been immediately under some considerable pressure and caught off balance, a plot on his life is even said to have been uncovered against him by a disgruntled Scythian who had deserted to the Romans but then escaped to the Pontic forces when he was discovered (App., *Mith.* 11.79; compare the more detailed account in Plutarch, *Luc.* 16). The historicity of the episode is rather suspect and again may simply be padding out a period of inactivity in military matters. A cause of delay may be attributed to the fact that Marcus Pomponius, the commander of the cavalry, had been captured in the engagement of the cavalry by the enemy. However, in typical Roman fashion, when brought before the king even though in pain from his wounds, when asked if he would be a friend to the king if Mithridates spared his life, he is said to have replied (Plut., *Luc.* 15.2) 'Yes indeed if you make peace with Rome otherwise I will remain your foe!' The king was suitably impressed with this remark and ordered that his injuries be cared for and that his life should be preserved. Meanwhile, the king's superiority in cavalry made Lucullus hesitant of moving his infantry from the relative safety of the hills.

Mithridates led out his forces from his camp and offered battle which Lucullus declined. Both our main sources agree that the Romans now looked for ways to outflank the enemy and so gain some advantage for what appears to be a grave miscalculation in the strength of their cavalry compared to the infantry. A fortuitous event occurred which gave Lucullus cause for an optimistic conclusion to his dilemma. Some Greeks were discovered hiding in a cave near the Roman encampment and one of these, named by Plutarch

(*Luc*. 15.3–4) as Artemidorus, promised to reveal to Lucullus a path which would take the Romans around their enemy and provide them with a new base from which it would be possible to launch attacks on Mithridates from the rear.[26] Appian is less specific than Plutarch and merely refers to some anonymous hunter (*Mith*. 12.80) who, found hiding in a cave, offered his services as a guide to Lucullus. Appian's account may perhaps be preferred.

Neither account is strictly credible since we are then asked to believe that the entire Roman army, or at least a major part of this, left its camp at night, leaving fires to divert the attention of any watchers from the Pontic side, and set off across mountainous tracks to arrive at another hilly location but this time to the rear of Mithridates. This seems a similar exercise to that engineered at Cyzicus and was actually a manoeuvre to cut off the enemy's escape. This would certainly have been the case had Lucullus divided his forces so that he now had two camps one before and one located at the rear of Mithridates' army. Neither Appian nor Plutarch was a military figure and so are not primarily concerned with tactics and here as elsewhere they give an incomplete picture on which we are forced to build or conjecture. Whatever, Lucullus' intention there was an immediate shortage of supplies to worry the general who sent for shipments of grain to be brought from Cappadocia. Meanwhile, a skirmish between the two sides developed into a more intense engagement and although the Pontic troops were initially pushed back, on the personal intervention of their king who urged them on they forced the Romans into a rout (App., *Mith*. 12.80) and they started to flee back to their camp. In Appian, Mithridates made the most of his unexpected victory by announcing the result far and wide, in Plutarch's account, in imitation of the king, Lucullus also intervened and (*Luc*. 15.7) the Romans turned this disaster into a victory. The troops who had run from the enemy were, however, punished by being forced to dig trenches in front of their fellow legionaries. Mithridates also seized the initiative in attempting to deny the Romans their badly needed supplies as had been imposed on him at Cyzicus. He therefore dispatched forces, twice in Plutarch's account (*Luc*. 17.1–2), to intercept these supply trains, but with no success at all. Appian says that the undisciplined Pontic cavalry failed to wait until it had the advantage of level ground, but instead attacked in the confines of a gully where the Romans were able to deploy their infantry to far better effect. The cavalry was hemmed in and then scattered with heavy losses. In Plutarch's account, both Pontic attacks related by him were repulsed with severe losses.[27] The king, when he learned about this latest reversal to the stronger military arm of his forces, immediately began to panic because he thought Lucullus would now launch a full-scale assault on his camp now that his cavalry had been decimated. Although the Romans did not do this, flight now dominated his thoughts and, it must be said, his behaviour is highly reminiscent of that seen in Antiochus III: violent mood swings, a personal participation in combat in the heroic mode, but a facile leadership with little planning or long-term strategy and an over-emotional or extremely charged reaction to any reverse when a cool calculated response would probably have saved the day or at least not contributed to a chaotic final outcome. It is of course necessary to remember that Roman writers of any age were likely to enhance the prestige of enemies to the state, and the seemingly amateurish nature of these opponents has to be seen in the context of their undoubted abilities as well. Yet here as at Cyzicus the reader is told that Mithridates again intended to escape without informing his troops which does not indicate a close bond between commander and common soldiers. He did inform his generals although this proved to be an unwise move. At Cyzicus the army commanders had been able to extract a sizable portion of the army from the siege to a safe beachhead at Lampsacus. In the wilds near Cabira no modicum of military discipline seems to have survived as the news leaked out that not only the king but also his senior advisors and officers were making a run for it. Even though it was after dark, it soon became obvious what was going on when wagons belonging to various court officials were seen leaving the gates of the camp. These gates quickly became congested as more and more individuals tried to depart taking their belongings with them. A melee soon developed and tempers frayed as the elite and the common soldiers – mostly conscripted peasants – by now completely panic stricken tried to get away. Although Mithridates had announced his intention to go he seems also to have somehow been delayed, and so was pitched into this heaving mass, as many of the soldiers sought to escape by tearing down the fortifications of the camp or tried to force their way out through the gates. Appian claims that the king attempted to calm fears, but was unseated from his horse; he managed to remount and so got away with a few close followers (App., *Mith.* 12.81). Plutarch again provides interesting additional detail claiming that Dorylaeus, one of Mithridates' generals, and Hermaeus, one of his senior priests, and Callistratus, his chief secretary, were all killed in the chaos. He also has the king fleeing on foot until a horse was provided for him by one of his court eunuchs, Ptolemaeus (*Luc.* 17.3–4). Appian has the king knocked down from his horse while trying to escape in the crush, but remounting and managing to get away with a small number of his household. The king's fortunes finally appeared to be in eclipse, and the end of war suddenly well in sight.

Chapter 9

Mithridates on the Run

... he was being chased by some Gauls, who did not realise
the identity of the fugitive, and he would have been captured,
if they had not come across a mule which was carrying
Mithridates' gold and silver, and had not stopped to plunder
this treasure.   (Memnon, *History of Heracleia* 30)

Mithridates' incredible good luck still held as he escaped the debacle at Cabira, and at once proceeded eastwards, first to the town of Comona, and then out of Pontus into Armenia. At some stage in this episode, either just before his departure or while he was still in flight, in the full realization that he had lost his kingdom, he ordered that his harem be killed even though it had been sent for safety to the city of Pharnacia on the coast away from the main theatre of war, but clearly to Mithridates now vulnerable to seizure by the Romans. Although in many respects a thoroughly Hellenized ruler, the king had several wives and concubines in his household, following the habit practised by the Persian monarchs from whom he was descended. Among these women, who included at least two Greek wives, were also family relations including, it is claimed, two sisters.[1] A eunuch named Bacchides was despatched to oversee the grisly task. The two Greek wives, Monimè and Berenice, were among the first to die, the first stabbed in the neck by Bacchides and the other strangled when the poison she had taken proved ineffective.[2] One of Mithridates' sisters died from poison, hurling curses down on his name. The other, Statira, died a quiet and dignified death, also from poison, absolving her brother from any wrongdoing and in fact praising his wisdom and care for ensuring that his female relatives were not taken alive by the enemy. It is said that Lucullus regretted such brutality (Plut., *Luc.* 18.6) but it must also be said that he would no doubt have displayed the women of Mithridates' household in any future triumph to the populace in Rome.

The Romans pursued Mithridates as far as Talaura where they missed the king and his entourage by as little as four days. After that, observing diplomatic protocol Lucullus proceeded no further, but occupied the towns and forts of Lower Armenia, and sent one of his officers, Appius Claudius Pulcher, to demand that Mithridates be handed over to him as a prisoner of war.[3] He then returned to Pontus to supervise clearing up operations of any remaining opposition. Lucullus is said to have taken Amastris and Heracleia, but was delayed for a brief time by Callimachus, the garrison commander at Amisus, who mounted a stout defence until Lucullus managed to storm the city. Sinope too held out against the Roman advance, but its fall appeared inevitable and those inhabitants who could, like the citizens of Amisus, escaped by ship. In a gesture of goodwill Lucullus reconstituted both these cities, and also made friendly overtures to Machares, Mithridates' son who ruled over the Cimmerian Bosporus. Lucullus then returned to the Roman province of Asia which certainly now needed more attention than ever following this period of protracted warfare, perhaps not fought out in the region itself but severely affecting its wealth and stability. Lucullus is said to have offered respite to the cities against excessive interest rates charged by mostly Roman and Italian merchants, and for this act he won the approval of the local communities but angered and estranged those who had power at home.[4] Those with influence at Rome stirred up opposition to Lucullus with the intention of reducing his political clout and with the ultimate aim of replacing him with one more amenable to their desires of making vast profits from the province. There was certainly agitation among political circles in Rome to have Lucullus' command terminated.

Meanwhile, Mithridates arrived in the kingdom of his son-in-law Tigranes with just 2,000 cavalrymen. Tigranes did not allow him to proceed to the royal court at Tigranocerta, perhaps wishing at this stage to be seen to be maintaining a level of neutrality in the war. This lukewarm reception may have come as a surprise to the Pontic king who had not long before successfully encouraged Tigranes to invade Cappadocia. Perhaps relations between them had cooled in the interim or because Tigranes was himself involved in a military campaign in Syria he did not want to allow his powerful father-in-law too much liberty while he was absent. So Mithridates was cordially welcomed, but confined to one of the royal estates, while Claudius Pulcher was instructed to meet the Armenian king at Antioch, a city he had recently occupied and an action which effectively ended the Seleucid rule of that region.[5] It seems that Pulcher's guides were under strict instructions to delay his progress as much as possible so that his arrival would coincide with that of Tigranes. However, the Roman envoy realizing that he was the victim of subterfuge dismissed his local escorts and made more rapid progress to Antioch than expected. There he had to wait for the return of the king who was further south and used the time to make further overtures to local magnates and various minor rulers whose future support or neutrality would be welcomed by Rome. Tigranes had not made himself popular with the Greeks of Syria, transplanting some to other parts of his kingdom and unwisely treating others with great disdain –

a situation advantageous to Rome. When Pulcher was finally admitted to a royal audience he told the king bluntly that Mithridates must be surrendered as a prize to Lucullus for victory over the Pontic monarch. The king rejected this request and stated that if attacked he would defend his lands. According to Plutarch (*Luc.* 22.1) it was only at this point that Tigranes allowed his father-in-law to meet him. They either met at Tigranocerta where the king had his palace or it is possible that Mithridates was invited to Antioch in the winter of 70/69 or, claims Appian, only some time later.[6] At this meeting it seems that Tigranes offered his father-in-law aid though perhaps not much more than moral support since repossession of the latter's kingdom, now lost, seemed an improbable wish to fulfil.

At the start of the spring in 69 Lucullus advanced into Armenia with a surprisingly small force, comprised says Appian (*Mith.* 12.84), of just two legions and only 500 cavalry. Plutarch (*Luc.* 24.2) gives a slightly larger total of 12,000 infantry (two legions) and 3,000 cavalry. Still this was hardly calculated to illustrate an impressive show of Roman power. The 'invasion' had been prompted by the fact that Tigranes had refused to hand over Mithridates to the Romans. Either it was a supreme example of reckless behaviour by the Roman commander, since this expeditionary force had to extract supplies from wherever it could and was clearly beyond the normal lines of communication which were usually established for any invading force; or Lucullus had simply come to show the flag, and expected Tigranes to back down without a fight. Appian says that the Armenian king was not even aware of a Roman invasion and that members of his court had clearly not thought to bother him with such details.[7] Lucullus on the other hand perhaps expected an easy and rapid victory.

When he did learn about this incursion, far from being intimidated by the Roman advance Tigranes decided to launch pre-emptive measures. This course is perhaps remarkable since he was surely well aware that since his father-in-law had been utterly defeated – and Mithridates had very good military credentials – then his fate was be likely to be similar. Still, one cannot account for human nature and especially the pride and warrior ethos of these Hellenistic kings. Indeed, it seems clear enough that Tigranes, perhaps in awe of Mithridates earlier in his reign, now sought to outdo him in glory, especially since he ignored the older man's warnings about engaging with the enemy too soon. Instead, Tigranes immediately ordered a commander named as Mithrobarzanes to harass Lucullus' column with 2,000 cavalry. The Romans ought to have expected such a response given the local predilection for cavalry warfare, but again Lucullus may have left himself rather exposed on this flank.[8] These were however repulsed with some ease it appears and the Armenian commander lost his life along with severe casualties among his troops.

At the same time Tigranes ordered that his capital at Tigranocerta be defended against attack setting a certain Mancaeus in command of the defence. The city was recently constructed but appears to have had solid defences yet the royal palace, perhaps in reality a former hunting lodge, lay outside the fortifications and was easily plundered by the Romans when they first arrived. Appian says that the Roman commander outside the city was Sextilius (*Mith.* 12.84), presumably a legate of Lucullus, and this was either an advance party or may indicate that the Romans had divided their forces at some point in their advance. According to Plutarch, Lucullus had indeed divided his available troops though the details are fuzzy and somewhat at odds with Appian's account. Sextilius had been the commander who, with a little more than 3,000 combined cavalry and light-armed troops, had successfully engaged and seen off the threat to the Roman column by Mithrobarzanes. And this same Sextilius had then prevented a large body of troops raised in Arabia from joining Tigranes' army (Plut., *Luc.* 25.5). Another of his legates, L. Licinius Murena (son of Sulla's legate), with unspecified forces, was sent to disrupt the general call to arms which had been issued by the king of Armenia.

Tigranes was actually gathering an army up country in person, a fact which must illustrate the rather haphazard and feudal nature of his resources, especially in terms of manpower, and that he had little in the way of a standing army. This is quite in contrast to other Hellenistic monarchs who maintained armies and also reservists in their cities. Indeed, until the later stages of his conflict with Rome Mithridates will have possessed a sizeable professional army including mercenaries, probably Greeks. Murena certainly appears to have been able to cause some considerable havoc inflicting both human and material losses to Tigranes who was intercepted somewhere in Armenia. Nonetheless, it is claimed that, despite these setbacks in his recruitment drive, he was still able to gather an immense force of 250,000 infantry and 50,000 cavalry, though how these were equipped or trained is anyone's guess, and the number is certainly highly questionable.[9] With this hastily levied army he marched to Tigranocerta. When he was near he sent ahead a force of 6,000 cavalry which broke through the Roman cordon. These, however, had been sent not to relieve the city, but on a specific mission: to rescue and bring away Tigranes' harem! By then Lucullus was also outside the city. The fact that his enemy was able to break in and then escape suggests that these 6,000 were sufficiently well trained to overcome Roman opposition twice, or that the besiegers were thinly spread and the cordon easily breached.

Tigranes by then was also approaching Tigranocerta with his new army and was keen to take the Romans on. Mithridates urged extreme caution and to concentrate on denying the enemy their supplies, as had been inflicted on him at Cyzicus. Mithridates' long-time general Taxiles lent his voice to this conservative strategy, but Tigranes was swayed by other advisers who suggested to him that the advice he was receiving from the Pontic faction was aimed at reducing his chances of greater glory. Moreover, and more to the point, the apparently insignificant size of Lucullus' force which was by then encamped close by was altogether too tempting to leave alone.

Tigranes held a position in the foothills of the Taurus Mountains overlooking Tigranocerta; Lucullus' camp was outside the city. The problem facing the Romans was whether to await the arrival of this huge Armenian army or to take to the offensive. Lucullus decided to be proactive, again dividing his available resources, leaving Murena with just 6,000 men to continue the investment of the city while he advanced against Tigranes. Lucullus made for a river which crossed a large plain in full view of his enemy; and Tigranes is said to have uttered the following: 'If they come as ambassadors they are too many, if as soldiers too few!' (Plut., *Luc.* 27.4). This king's hubris was shortly to meet its nemesis in the might of Rome as had happened to so many other rulers who had chosen to defy what had almost become an inevitability in the ancient Mediterranean.

From the heights Lucullus was seen to strike camp, moving north away from the Armenian host and seemingly in retreat. Tigranes was naturally delighted and gleefully summoned Taxiles to witness his victory without there being any need to engage at all. It was at this point that the veteran general of the recent wars enlightened the king, who was clearly ignorant about Roman battle etiquette, that if the Romans were indeed withdrawing they would neither be in battle gear nor would they be drawn up in strict formation. A river, one of the tributaries of the Tigris, separated the two sides, with Tigranes on the east bank and the Romans on the west. The river made a turn to the west where it was fordable and it was in this direction that Lucullus led his troops. He was the first to cross this stream, with the intention of wheeling around to take the opposition on the flank (see Map 8). Tigranes was taken completely by surprise, and hurriedly drew up his line of battle to face this unexpected Roman move. He was now facing the Romans who were moving southwards but still uphill, with himself in command of the centre, the king of the Adiabeni to his left, and a king of the Medes to his right (Plut., *Luc.* 27.6). At some point Lucullus was told that this particular day, 6 October, was an unlucky one, a *dies nefasti*, since this was the date in 105 that the Romans had suffered a catastrophic defeat at Arausio at the hands of the Cimbri, where 80,000 Romans and allied troops had been killed.[10] Lucullus' response was: 'in which case I will also make this day a lucky one for the Romans!' (Plut., *Luc.* 27.7).

The Roman plan was for a rapid assault, assuming that the Armenian army would be slow to face around for this charge, bringing the legionaries quickly into close-quarter combat at which they were most effective and also reducing the chance of enemy archers taking a high toll. The distance between the two forces was a mere 4 stades, says Plutarch (*Luc.* 28.2), a little more than half a mile (800 metres). Allied cavalry drawn from Thracian and Gallic (Galatian) allies were to attack the Armenian flanks and to immobilize the cataphracts, whose heavy and inflexible armour, which covered both rider and horse, made their manoeuvring difficult and suspect when faced with the sort of spontaneous and sporadic yet agile attack methods employed by the lighter armed troops. Lucullus himself led two cohorts – probably again cavalry – while the infantry followed behind, and he occupied the hill, his objective, before the enemy could even draw up. He then ordered the enemy cataphracts on the left and right wings to be attacked and these appear to have started the rout as they tried to escape through the lines of their own infantry now drawn up behind them. Great slaughter is said to have taken place, which is hardly surprising since the Roman force was made up of veteran soldiers, their opponents for the most part of raw levies. Tigranes deserted the field of battle within a few minutes and fled with a small group of attendants. He passed his diadem to his son as if surrendering his kingship and urged the young man to seek out another way of escape. This young man handed the diadem to a slave for safe-keeping and that slave was captured by the Romans and with him the diadem of the Armenian king.

> It is claimed that 100,000 of the enemy's infantry was killed while of the cavalry only a few escaped. On the Roman side there were just five fatalities and 100 injured.   (Plut., *Luc.* 28.6)

Appian (*Mith.* 12.85–86) has far less detail and different material about the battle outside Tigranocerta than does Plutarch who is mainly keen to portray Lucullus in the best possible light. Appian or his source simply notes Lucullus' competence as a general and rather focuses on the poor leadership of Tigranes. Mithridates is again made to suggest, in reasonable fashion, avoiding battle; advice which Tigranes, another would-be Achilles, unwisely rejected with scorn, drawing up his army for battle immediately. Pointedly, in Appian the Roman cavalry is made to be employed to draw the enemy forward, while the infantry bypassed the Armenian army entirely and took up position on the hill behind their enemy's line from which they could launch an attack from the rear.

> When he saw how few the Romans were he ridiculed them saying: 'If they come as envoys there are too many, if they come as enemies far too few.' Lucullus saw a hill which was usefully situated behind Tigranes and so he positioned his cavalry for an immediate charge to harass the opposition and draw the enemy out against the Romans who were to retreat in order so that the barbarians would in pursuit

break their own ranks while unobserved he led his infantry around the hill and occupied it. When he saw the Armenian army pursuing his cavalry as if they were the victors scattered all over the battlefield and their camp at the foot of the hill he shouted 'Men we are victorious!' and raced down against the camp followers. Immediately these fled and ran up against their own infantry who in turn collided with their cavalry. In a moment the rout was complete.

The Roman cavalry, as planned, suddenly wheeled about and fell on their hapless pursuers, who were cut down mercilessly. The Armenian king's troops were encircled and in trying to escape were crowded together and slaughtered. Lucullus had ordered that no plunder was to be taken until after the battle was won and so the killing continued until nightfall, by which time the Romans had pursued their opponents for a distance of 120 stades (between 14 and 15 miles). Only then were the legionaries recalled and the collection of war spoils began. The Armenian king's horror and panic is again graphically captured as his baggage train was overwhelmed, the carriers driven against the infantry and these troops against their own cavalry, with resultant chaos. Ancient writers commented on the fact that this victory was remarkable because it had been won by a Roman army vastly outnumbered by its opponents: probably less than 10,000 troops had been available to Lucullus, while ancient accounts, even if they give an exaggerated total for Tigranes, have his army in excess of 200,000.[11] Lucullus was an outstanding general but he also commanded seasoned and well trained forces, while his enemy though powerful in number was no match for organisation and reasoned tactics.[12]

In Appian's account Tigranocerta also immediately fell to the Romans, but in Plutarch this climax is deemed hardly a mention (*Luc.* 29.1–2). It is apparent that the position of Mancaeus, the commander inside the city, had obviously become critical. In fear that his Greek mercenary troops would either desert or mutiny, he had them disarmed. These then had gathered together for self-protection, armed only with clubs, when Mancaeus ordered their immediate execution and sent his own troops to carry out this order. The plan backfired badly:

> They wound their cloaks around their left arms to act as shields and courageously ran against their attackers and at once shared out among themselves the arms of those they killed. With the arms they had provided for themselves they occupied a part of the walls between some towers and called to the Romans outside who were admitted when they ran up. (Appian, *Mith.* 12.86)

Once the Romans had gained a foothold inside the fortifications, Tigranocerta was quickly captured and sacked to the tune of 8,000 talents, while Lucullus

reserved the royal treasures for himself. He also liberally rewarded his troops
with a bonus of 800 denarii a piece, celebrated magnificent games in the city
and returned to their native cities those Greeks who had been forced to migrate
there and any other displaced persons. Tigranocerta, populated with those
subjected to enforced removal, was therefore denuded of its inhabitants, and
the Romans gained much popularity by this action.

Plutarch suggests that Mithridates had not been present at the battle but that
the two kings met only afterwards, and openly declared their support' for one
another; and immediately went about raising another army, the command
of which Tigranes handed over to his father-in-law. Mithridates personally
supervised the selection of the best available men, about 70,000 infantry and
35,000 cavalry says Appian (*Mith.* 13.87), and their training, which was based
heavily on the Roman system of cohorts, and equipment for his infantry
modelled on that of the legionary. Tigranes, apparently so suspicious of his
father-in-law beforehand, now left him in complete control of all military
affairs and went to his palace at Artaxata in Central Armenia. His possible aim
was to open negotiations with the Parthian king about military aid. Phraates III
(70–57 BC) had recently succeeded to the Parthian throne and was either a
subtle diplomat or, assessing the probable negative consequences of getting
involved, was also open to Roman overtures. To both sides he promised aid in
return for future material gains (Mesopotamia was demanded from Tigranes as
the price for aid), but he made no particular attempt to commit himself.
Lucullus had already had some diplomatic successes with other states in the
regions – Plutarch names these as the Arabs, Sopheni and Gordyeni (*Luc.*
29.5–6) – a pact with the Parthian king would have been of immense propaganda value to the Roman commander and a further feather in his cap.
However, the Romans soon learned that Phraates was playing a devious game.
Lucullus retaliated by deciding that a further campaign against Mithridates
and Tigranes was less important than one against the Parthians and he issued
orders for the army stationed in Pontus to join him. The garrison stationed
there was commanded by the legate Sornatius (Plut., *Luc.* 30.3),[13] and he found
that his soldiers were simply not interested in fighting any longer. For them
the war was over or so they thought – how wrong they were! When the troops
accompanying Lucullus heard this news they too, for the most part, also
refused to contemplate the invasion of a state even more remote from their
homes.

Lucullus was obliged to accede to the demands of his troops, and so moved
northwards against Tigranes in the summer of 68. The details of this campaigning season are rather disjointed in the sources and not easily reconciled.
Appian's account is the more straightforward but he clearly misses important
events which are luckily relayed by Plutarch whose focus is Lucullus' actions

rather than the war. Still, it is quite clear that not only was there no final Roman triumph but there were actually setbacks. These may have been caused by the remote terrain, on the one hand, and on the other the lack of enthusiasm by the Roman forces to pursue an objective which had become the capture or permanent elimination of both Mithridates and Tigranes.[14] An attempt to force a single battle with the enemy did not succeed and although an attack made by Tigranes on Lucullus' column was seen off, Mithridates avoided an engagement with the Roman which he must surely have known he would lose. Appian claims that the forces of the two kings was meant to encircle the Roman army but that Lucullus used his cavalry to prevent Tigranes deploying his force in battle formation. Mithridates is said to have constructed a camp from which he would not venture and although besieged by the Romans the arrival of winter forced their withdrawal because of a lack of supplies. Tigranes retreated to Artaxata. Plutarch says that Lucullus marched after Tigranes and that the Armenian came to meet him with a force mostly of cavalry. The River Arsania separated the two forces and to get at their enemy the Romans were forced to cross. The Roman centre consisted of just twelve cohorts with cavalry cover on the flanks, the Armenian wings comprised mercenaries named as Mardian mounted archers and Iberian cavalry armed with spears (Plut., *Luc.* 31.5). These appear to have immediately broken and fled before the Roman assault and Lucullus' cavalry took off in pursuit. Tigranes in person led his own cavalry towards the Roman centre and although initially apprehensive about the capacity of the enemy Lucullus recalled his own cavalry and led his infantry against the king's entourage. The Armenian centre is said to have collapsed quite rapidly and that in the rout:

> ... the Romans were exhausted not only because of the number of enemy they killed but also from taking prisoners and acquiring many sorts of plunder. Livy says that in the previous battle there had been great numbers of enemy casualties but that in this one more elite figures were killed and taken captive.   (Plut., *Luc.* 31.8)

Plutarch has Mithridates present in this battle but Appian has him far away and re-entering Pontus with about 8,000 troops where, with considerable audacity, he out-marshalled C. Fabius Hadrianus the legate left in charge by Lucullus. Fabius lost 500 men and would have been annihilated had Mithridates not been seriously wounded in the fighting which had resumed on a second day.[15] Fabius then received reinforcements from troops led by Valerius Triarius who also took over the command and with Mithridates apparently fully restored to health the fighting began again. This battle was interrupted by a storm and hurricane-like winds and forced both sides to regroup. However, when Triarius learned that Lucullus was not far away and moving to join him he decided to force Mithridates into another fight, perhaps hoping for sole glory over the Pontic king or possibly assuming that the enemy was no longer as formidable as it had once been. Triarius was greatly mistaken in his assumptions since the fight was tough and Mithridates used his superiority in cavalry to overrun the Roman infantry which scattered but was caught in muddy ditches where it became easy prey. A Roman rout seemed inevitable until Mithridates was again wounded this time in the thigh, says Appian (*Mith.* 13.89), by a centurion who had been running alongside the king's horse. The king was hurriedly carried from the field and his soldiers were recalled from their pursuit of the Romans who very fortunately made their escape although with heavy casualties. Mithridates' life again lay in the balance, until the loss of blood was contained by Timotheus his personal physician.[16] Yet within the same day Mithridates was back in command and in pursuit of the Romans who, nonetheless, managed to escape due to the hiatus in the fighting. Appian claims that 24 military tribunes and 150 centurions had been killed. This figure is impossible for the sort of numbers of troops who could have been under the command of Triarius and Hadrianus and is used to emphasise the magnitude but also the un-expectedness of the defeat at this late stage in the war.[17]

In Central Armenia, Lucullus had not been able to follow up his victory against Tigranes because of the early onset of winter storms in the second half of September, which made it almost impossible to advance as the army was hampered by deep snow and icy conditions. Further unhappiness among the troops about the constant campaigning also made itself heard in complaints delivered to their commander by the officers, but finally in almost open mutiny. Lucullus personally endeavoured to persuade his soldiers to carry on towards Artaxata, but he was unsuccessful and obliged to withdraw.[18] He moved south into Mygdonia where the land was warm and fertile and where the city of Nisibis was situated. If he could not take Artaxata Lucullus would have Nisibis instead. A brother of Tigranes named Gouras held the command at Nisibis but it was the Greek Callimachus, previously in charge at Amisus, who engineered its defence. The Romans were not to be denied this prize and the city quickly fell. Callimachus was captured and probably executed, unlike Gouras who was detained but well treated. It seemed as if Lucullus' winning streak was indeed to continue. However, his troops although successful at Nisibis remained unruly and uncooperative, and the complaints continued un-abated. Their main grievance was that Lucullus refused to allow his legionaries comfortable winter quarters in a friendly city and instead they were always kept confined to their camps. Many of these troops had served in Asia since the first war with Mithridates, and they wanted to go home. These found a spokesman in a young man who acquired a certain degree of notoriety in Roman political life in the late 60s and 50s, a relative of Lucullus by marriage, his name Publius

Clodius Pulcher. The ancient sources are almost entirely hostile towards Clodius and Plutarch is no exception, with little good to say about this figure who he says stirred up the troops against Lucullus and used the situation to further his own political career. Yet Clodius was not penalized for his so-called perfidious activities. He may have been a close relative of Lucullus and was brother to one of Lucullus' previous legates, but had his intentions been mutinous he would certainly not have been able to pursue a successful political career so soon afterwards. It is likely therefore that adverse propaganda had crept into the source material and been recounted by Plutarch.[19] Whatever the source and its intent, the situation brought a standstill to Lucullus' campaign and his army spent the winter of 67 in Gordyene where his troops confidently expected a change in commander.

Plutarch says (*Luc.* 35.1) that it was only now that Lucullus heard of the defeat of Fabius Hadrianus and that Mithridates was moving against Sornatius and Triarius, and soon after that the defeat of Triarius. This sufficiently shamed Lucullus' soldiers into following him although they arrived too late to be of any use to their defeated comrades. A witch-hunt for Triarius by disgruntled troops was foiled by Lucullus but he had great difficulty in persuading his men to follow Mithridates who, with winter approaching, now retreated into Lesser Armenia to the south east of Pontus, desolating the countryside as he went in order to compound Lucullus' problems were he to follow. As it was, although Lucullus tried to entice Mithridates into battle, the latter was not deceived as to his chances of success, even faced with mutinous Roman troops, and decided to wait for reinforcements from Tigranes. Lucullus aimed to intercept the Armenian king and so prevent the two kings from joining their forces, but he was destined not to engage in battle again. Many of his troops refused to take further orders from him and although they did not abandon their camp they would only take up arms again if confronted with an enemy attack. According to Plutarch (*Luc.* 35.5) Tigranes now launched a raiding attack on Cappadocia while Mithridates was able to undermine Roman control in Pontus. Lucullus had received orders to disband his army and return to Rome. The majority of the forces under his command followed the instructions sent via the Roman governor of Asia. Lucullus was also informed that he had been accused at Rome of needlessly prolonging the war with Pontus. He would have to answer these charges once he arrived back in Italy. The knockout blow simply could not be administered, and so Mithridates VI, still the king of Pontus, lived to fight another day.

> Thus it happened that Lucullus' war against Mithridates like those which had previously occurred, did not reach a fixed and certain ending. (App., *Mith.* 14.91)

Chapter 10

Mithridates and Pompey the Great

Plutarch in his biography of Pompey the Great has this to say about the start of his subject's involvement in the war against Mithridates VI of Pontus.

> When it became known in Rome that the war against the pirates had been ended and that Pompey was not now committed to any further business in this matter but was then visiting various cities in the East, Manilius, one of the tribunes of the plebs, introduced a law transferring to Pompey the provincial command and army of Lucullus, plus Bithynia, then under the command of Glabrio.[1] The task was specified as undertaking a war against the kings Mithridates and Tigranes.
> (Plut., *Pomp.* 30)

Pompey's appointment against Mithridates followed hard on his successful war against piracy throughout the Mediterranean. Piracy was endemic to the ancient Mediterranean world, but Rome's wars with Pontus had exacerbated this problem. On the one hand the seas were not being sufficiently well policed because of the pressing need to focus on the campaigns against Mithridates and, on the other hand, the Pontic monarch had seen in these various pirate bands useful allies and so had encouraged their illicit activities. The result was a tremendous upsurge in their attacks. The Aegean Sea had certainly become an unsafe place, but even Italy and the very hub of the Roman Empire were not immune to such incursions. Pirates are recorded as being active in Sicilian waters towards the end of the 70s, including an audacious raid on the city of Syracuse. These caused such immense disruption to shipping, particularly of the vital imports of grain, that a famine threatened Rome itself in 67. This quite clearly prompted the passage of a plebiscite – a law passed by the plebeian assembly but binding on the whole community – to award Pompey an extensive command to put down this menace. The law was proposed by the tribune A. Gabinius,[2] a long-standing friend of Pompey's, and it stipulated that:

> Pompey's authority was to extend over the whole sea right up to the Pillars of Hercules and over all land up to 400 stades (80km) from the coast.[3] In addition he was allowed to select fifteen senatorial legates

for various positions of command. He was granted funds from the
treasury and allowed such money from the *publicani* as he required.[4]
He was granted 200 ships and the power to levy as many soldiers and
rowers as he needed.   (Plut., *Pomp*. 25)

The people threatened with food shortages were wildly enthusiastic about this
proposal, some members of the senate much less so because they saw in it,
rightly too, the sort of legislation which could undermine a collective system
of government. Indeed, the day after the initial proposals had been voted, a
personal appearance by Pompey led to the number of ships being increased to
500 and the troops at his disposal to 24 legates, 120,000 infantry and 5,000
cavalry. Pompey was, therefore, in a strong position from the beginning and
proved to be extremely efficient in his commission for within three months he
was able to announce that the waters of 'Mare Nostrum' were again open for
civilian shipping. At the climax of his campaign he had pursued pirates into
their fortresses in Cilicia where the town of Coracesium was evidently a notable
centre (Plut., *Pomp*. 28). When these surrendered the ex-pirates to the tune of
20,000 were resettled in various parts of Cilicia including the cities of Soli and
Dyme.

    With this war concluded, the Roman voting population was easily convinced
that Pompey was the ideal general to bring an end at last to the conflict with
Mithridates. Lucullus' long command had for some time become unpopular
although it was by no means an unusually lengthy stint. Pompey himself had
spent between five and six years in Spain (late 77 to the end of 72), and his
fellow commander Q. Caecilius Metellus Pius a whole decade.[5] It was rather a
concatenation of events which brought not only the neglect of the sea lanes, but
also his rather aloof and arrogant manner which had eroded support in the
senate and especially among the people – the very ones who provided from
their ranks the soldiers who fought under his command. It became easy enough
for men to say that he was dawdling over the outcome of the war to suit his own
desires for greater glory and for such propaganda to be believed. Of course, the
main critics of Pompey at this time, and those who still supported Lucullus
stressed the point that the former general here had all but completed his task
and that Pompey was simply left with tidying up operations and would then be
able to claim the credit for finishing the war. This was not the first time that
such a thing had occurred and it must certainly have reminded some of Marius'
appointment against Jugurtha, the king of Numidia, in 107 in much the same
circumstances, arguments and procedure.[6]

    Pompey was still in Asia when he was granted the command by an over-
whelming vote and a new plebiscite steered by the tribune Manilius, a political
ally, gave him wide powers.[7] He received this new commission by letter.

Pompey's response is reported by Plutarch, probably from a history of the campaigns by Theophanes of Mytilene, who was a friend of Pompey and accompanied the general in Asia Minor.

> 'Is there no end in sight to my labours? It really is best if one is born an unknown. Look at me! My service in the army will never come to an end and I shall never be able to shake off the envy that accompanies my success and live quietly with my wife in the country.'
>
> (Plut., *Pomp.* 30)

In reality Pompey certainly coveted this command and, as he is supposed to have hated Lucullus, no doubt looked on this as being a double triumph over a long-standing political opponent.[8] Of course, the command may be seen as a gift of thanks to Pompey given by the Roman people for removing the threat of famine which had become almost a reality because of the proliferation of piracy even in Rome's own backyard. However, there was much opposition to the transfer of the war's progress from Lucullus, although he had been in the region for eight years. There had never been a rule written or unwritten that a senator appointed to a command should always finish the brief, indeed it was precisely against the holding of long term commands which had governed traditional practices. Yet there was grave disquiet among many senators who saw Pompey's grant of yet another immense *imperium* as a possible platform from which to leap to sole power in the state. Supporters of Pompey, including Cicero, could argue quite cogently that there had been long term commands with wide-ranging powers before, including that of Scipio Africanus' command in Spain and then his supervision of the Roman invasion of Africa leading to the battle of Zama and defeat of Hannibal in 202. His adopted grandson Scipio Aemilianus had been elected consul below the legal age for the office and had been appointed to the command against Carthage in 147. He was then still in his thirties and eligible only for the aedileship. The argument which prevailed was that exceptional circumstances called for a special command, and that Rome was greater and stronger than any individual's ambition. In the case of Pompey this argument proved to be correct but, in the long term, it failed to contain the still greater ambitions of Julius Caesar and later his heir Octavian who became the first Roman emperor as Augustus in 27 BC.

Still in 67 the *lex Manilia* by which Pompey obtained his new command was quite specific in its aims: to put an end at the earliest opportunity to the war with Mithridates. Although the Pontic king can hardly have been in as powerful a position as the one he had possessed in the 90s or just prior to his invasion of Bithynia in 74, his powers of recuperation certainly appear remarkable if we are to believe our sources. According to Appian (*Mith.* 14.91) Mithridates had taken the opportunity in the hiatus caused by the termination of Lucullus' command, the inactivity of his army or its dispersal, and Pompey's arrival in the theatre of war, still in Cilicia, to take up his command to attack Cappadocia and to some extent restore his power in Pontus. He also suggests that Mithridates was able to take advantage of Roman preoccupation with the pirate menace, although this cannot be historically accurate seeing that Lucullus and later several other senior commanders including Pompey were in Asia by 67.[9] The stamping out of the piracy problem does not seem to have impacted negatively on Mithridates' fortunes which were brought low by the relentless campaigning of Lucullus. However, with the pirates removed from the equation the Roman focus against one of its most wily foes inevitably became keener than before; and the military capability available to Pompey far exceeded that allowed to his immediate predecessor or indeed any other general who had fought Mithridates.

Pompey moved his considerable forces from the province of Asia to Pontus where Mithridates was waiting. Appian appears to suggest (*Mith.* 15.97) that although the king had good reserves of manpower on which to call, at the same time he had great difficulty in maintaining his troops and keeping them disciplined and loyal. A force of just 30,000 infantry and 3,000 cavalry was quite paltry in comparison to the vast host he had previously been able to command. Still, the devastation caused by Lucullus meant that supplies were not easily available, and it is likely that essential materials such as arms were also inadequate. Desertions had, therefore, evidently become a commonplace.

> The deserters he caught were either crucified, or had their eyes gouged out or were burned alive. Yet although the fear of punishment reduced the numbers of those deserting, the lack of provisions weakened his men.   (App., *Mith.* 15.97)

Pompey had a huge advantage and Mithridates was understandably reluctant to offer battle, and even sought terms although the Romans expected nothing less than unconditional surrender, which the king refused to contemplate. Some skirmishing took place in which Mithridates had the upper hand but had to retreat because of his lack of supplies and Pompey was allowed to enter Pontus unopposed. Lucullus' army had already devastated the area, which contributed greatly to the problems of Mithridates, and if he thought that this would also hamper Pompey's advance he was to be sadly mistaken since the Roman supply lines were well organized, the lines of communication fully integrated into Pompey's strategy. Still, Mithridates took up a strong position which Pompey then put under siege by encircling the camp. This siege lasted forty-five days until the Pontic forces, again without adequate provisions, fled overnight to be pursued by the Romans.

The chase ended at the River Euphrates and Mithridates is said to have been forewarned of the outcome in a dream (Plut., *Pomp*. 32.3–4) and was actually woken by his officers as Pompey ordered a night attack across the river. Pompey is said to have adopted this fairly unusual but not unique tactic because he feared a similar attack from Mithridates. He need not have worried! Although the Pontic army had time to form up in front of its camp and although Pompey was hesitant considering the dangers of making night attacks which potentially could easily end badly for the offensive side, he was convinced by his advisers that he could succeed.[10] There was a setting moon behind the Romans which threw the defenders because they were unable to gauge correct distances for the archers or javelin throwers and even attacked shadows. Panic quickly set in and a rout began, Mithridates' camp was taken and he lost at least 10,000 men, according to Plutarch (*Pomp*. 32.7), but the king escaped with about 800 cavalry and made his way to a town named Sinora, possibly close to the border with Armenia.[11] From there his troops were dispersed and he initially intended heading into Armenia to seek sanctuary with Tigranes, but was turned back and forbidden to enter that kingdom. Indeed a 100-talent prize was placed on his head by his son-in-law. Mithridates therefore avoided this place, and instead marched along the coastal plain into Colchis where he spent the winter of 66 at Dioscurias. It is claimed that he then first contemplated going overland around the Euxine Sea, expelling his son Machares from his kingdom in the Crimea and then invading the Roman Empire from the north via the Danube and Thrace. Dioscurias was certainly en route to the Crimea, and was even closer by ship, so the story is perhaps not such a fanciful one as Appian supposes (*Mith*. 15.101). The intention of the story is surely to highlight the beginning of the king's descent into madness and despair. Yet he did precisely this journey by land and took possession of the Crimea, and in particular its chief city Panticapaeum (modern Kertsch), at the mouth of the Sea of Azov. Machares, his son, committed suicide when he learned of his father's approach.

Pompey also advanced into Colchis, but missed Mithridates who escaped the Romans yet again. At this point, Pompey's expedition takes on something of the feel of an odyssey in which he meets and fights nomadic tribes on the furthest reaches of the known world, including a meeting with Amazon warriors. This material is clearly intended as a positive comparison with the campaigns of Alexander in the East; and it obviously emanated from the stylus of Theophanes who cast himself into the role of court historian in much the same way that Callisthenes of Olynthus, nephew of Aristotle, had fulfilled an identical role for Alexander. Thus:

> Leaving Afranius in command of Armenia, going by the one accessible route which was possessed by tribes who lived near the Caucasus

Mountains, Pompey went in pursuit of Mithridates.[12] The largest of these tribes are called Albanians and Iberians. At first, the Albanians agreed that Pompey should be allowed to pass unmolested through their lands, but when the Romans were still in this region in the winter and were celebrating the Saturnalia the Albanians collected an army of at least forty thousand men and attacked having crossed the Cyrnus River. Pompey led his army against them and causing severe casualties put them to rout. However, when their king sent envoys to plead for clemency Pompey was conciliatory and made a treaty with the Albanians. He next marched against the Iberians ... these too were defeated by Pompey in a tremendous battle in which they lost nine thousand men and more than ten thousand were taken prisoner.

Pompey received news that the Albanians had again rebelled, news which angered him. He determined that these should not hold him in contempt and so he returned and crossed the Cyrnus. Crossing this river was difficult and dangerous ... and he then had to make long marches through arid and unfriendly country. For this campaign he had ten thousand skins filled with water and so arrived at the Abas River where he found his enemy drawn up for battle. They had sixty thousand infantry and twelve thousand cavalry, but had insufficient arms ... they were led by their king, a man named Cosis, who charged at Pompey when the armies clashed and struck him with a spear in the joint of his breastplate, but Pompey killed him with a sword thrust.

It is said that Amazons were also fighting on the side of the Albanians and that they had come to this place from the mountains near the Thermodon River. Indeed the Romans found shields and greaves favoured by the Amazons when they were collecting the battle spoils but found no bodies. The Amazons live in certain regions of the Caucasus Mountains where it descends to the Hyrcanian Sea. The land of the Amazons does not lie adjacent to that of the Albanians for the Gelae and Leges live in between, and the Amazons meet these tribes every year near the Thermodon River and stay with them for two months before returning to their own homeland.

(Plut., *Pomp.* 34–35)

Theophanes must have used the works of writers about Alexander as sources for enhancing the reputation and glory of Pompey in what was probably a rather sordid campaign against ill-armed tribes. The killing in single combat of the enemy leader Cosis is plainly an attempt to glorify Pompey who elsewhere is not particularly remembered as a general who craved being in the thick of things, but who rather liked to manage his command from a distance. The story is in any case certainly unhistorical and the creation of Theophanes, whose history Plutarch certainly had access to (Plut., *Pomp*. 37.3). Yet the propaganda undoubtedly did its job since Pompey's title, 'the Great', caused many even in Antiquity to view him as the Roman Alexander. And Pompey seems to have considered going by the overland route to the Cimmerian Bosporus (Crimea) providing that the opposition to his advance was not too intense; but the attack at the Saturnalia (January 65 BC) and the subsequent heavy fighting probably convinced him that it was neither a very feasible nor, seeing that Mithridates no longer posed much threat, a sensible option. He may well have also considered shipping his troops by sea since he rendezvoused with his commander of the fleet, Servilius, at some unspecified harbour on the eastern shores of the Euxine (Plut., *Pomp*. 34.5).[13] In the end Pompey evidently had second thoughts about the whole notion of an invasion of the Crimea since he is next placed in Amisus in Pontus.

In this campaign Pompey had evidently been accompanied by one of Tigranes's sons, also named Tigranes, who hoped to replace his father, and who had the support of Phraates, the Parthian king, to whom he was related by marriage. The elder Tigranes had no fight left in him, however, and arrived at Pompey's camp, by then near Artaxata, where he was received with unexpected warmth and allowed to retain his kingdom, although it is suggested by both Plutarch and Appian that hefty bribes (Plutarch) or gifts (Appian) were needed to accomplish this. It is said that Pompey's favour was bought with the princely sum of 6,000 talents while his officers and every single legionary each received handsome amounts to secure their good will as well. Quite clearly bribing the entire army would be necessary in order that Tigranes' city of Artaxata should escape the fate of Tigranocerta, still recent in everyone's minds. The elder Tigranes could continue to rule in Armenia, while his son was granted Lesser Armenia, also known as Sophene and Gordyene (App., *Mith*. 15.105). Of course, the result of these negotiations thwarted the grander ambitions of the younger Tigranes who had hoped to replace his father. He made no secret of his disgust at Pompey's actions and was promptly arrested, lost his newly allotted realm and completely disappears from history. Phraates meanwhile demanded that the young man be returned to him and that the River Euphrates was recognised as the border between Roman and Parthian spheres of influence. Pompey refused both requests.[14]

In the mean time, Panticapaeum did not prove to be the safe sanctuary that Mithridates had hoped for and his declining fortunes were made more problematic by plots and dissatisfaction within his own family. Those closest to the king probably realized that his end could not be far away. And such feelings would have increased when he sent envoys to Pompey, who was not at all conciliatory. Pompey instructed Mithridates' envoys to convey to their king the message that he must come in person to Amisus and plead his case before the Roman general for retaining his kingdom. This course of action Mithridates thought demeaning and refused to even to consider, but at the same time started to levy a new army. Another of his sons, named Xiphares by Appian, was executed, after being urged on to betray his father by his mother Stratonice, for attempting to desert to Pompey with valuables of his father which had been stored for safe keeping in a local fortress. But even with these resources Mithridates was forced to exact crippling tribute from the cities of this region in order to pay for arms, siege machines and timber for warships.[15] Although he collected an army said to have been in excess of 35,000 men he was unable to take the strategically important town of Phanagoria across the strait from Panticapaeum. His forces had evidently already seized the town's citadel for several of his children were in residence there, but Castor who was apparently a prominent citizen led a rebellion and successfully excluded the king's forces, led by one of his eunuchs, Trypho, from taking the town and relieving the garrison. Four sons and a daughter of Mithridates – Eupatra, Artaphernes, Xerxes, Darius and Oxathres – are said to have surrendered to the besiegers who were handed over to the Romans unharmed.[16] Another daughter named as Cleopatra held out in the fortress and was rescued by her father when he sent a squadron of ships across the strait expressly for this purpose. The events at Phanagoria had the effect of causing a more widespread revolt against the king, while he considered his army's loyalty highly dubious. He therefore contrived a quite remarkable gamble, one born out of desperation, of sending his unmarried daughters under escort to the neighbouring Scythian tribes promising these as wives in return for military aid. This venture too came to nothing since the eunuchs in charge of the company were murdered by their troops who instead took the King's daughters to Pompey.

Nonetheless, Mithridates was still not willing to give up the fight just yet, and turned his thoughts to an invasion of Italy by way of the Danube valley and Illyria. He had heard tales of how the wounds of the recent civil war in Italy had yet to heal and where he might just conceivably obtain support if he was able to march an army into the peninsula. Such a story is quite incredible, especially that he should entertain such notions and that the Italian allies would prefer the rule of a Hellenistic autocrat to that of the Romans! Still he seems to have taken this idea seriously or was by then sufficiently deluded into believing such a plan possible, perhaps spurred on by the flattery of his courtiers. It does also suggest that his formerly iron grip on reality was failing fast – he was by then approaching his seventieth year and had been king for nearly sixty of those years. His soldiers were unhappy but initially did nothing. His favourite son and designated successor Pharnaces now also considered that the time had come to plot against his father. The conspiracy was exposed and those associated with the prince apprehended and executed but Pharnaces himself was spared through the intercession of a counsellor named as Menophanes (App., *Mith.* 16.110). Mithridates had deviated from his usually sound, if brutally realistic, view of life, and so he was caught unprepared when Pharnaces launched a second attempt to wrest power from his parent. This was to be no secret conspiracy but a simple insinuation of the king's troops already uneasy about his grandiose plans to attack Rome. Pharnaces worked his charms, probably with bribes, firstly on Roman deserters who realized the risks entailed in an expedition from the Bosporus to Italy and who had the most to lose if they were captured by their compatriots. Immediate execution awaited deserters who had enlisted as mercenaries with the enemy if taken prisoner in a battle. It appears that these then suborned others among the Pontic army. The mutiny took a firm hold among numerous sections of the army and among the fleet, not surprisingly considering the current fortunes of Mithridates, who became aware of a general disturbance in his camp one morning and sent messengers to inquire about the reason. These received the blunt response:

'We want your son to be the king, and we want a young man not one who is old and governed by eunuchs, a killer of his sons, his generals and his friends.'   (App., *Mith.* 16.110)

Mithridates himself went to try and regain the confidence of his troops, but his own guards ran off to join the deserters in the camp. These however were refused admission unless they showed themselves to be really honest in their intentions, the implication being, if any was needed, that they should kill the king. Mithridates got away back to his palace, but his horse had been killed in the melee that developed outside the camp, and it became clear that support was quickly draining away from the monarch. He sent several messengers – one wonders from where he could still draw supporters – to his son asking for permission to go into exile. Pharaces wisely did not reply nor did he allow the messengers to return to his father. Mithridates now afraid of being taken alive and delivered to Pompey decided to commit suicide by taking poison. It is said that in his company were two young daughters who demanded that they also be given the poison so that they might die with him. He agreed to this bizarre request but while the young girls quickly succumbed to the effects of the drug, he was unaffected, possibly because the quantity was too small or from possessing natural antibodies in his bloodstream. It is claimed that constantly fearful of being poisoned he had experimented in taking small quantities of all poisons then known so that he would become immune to their effects. After some time he turned to one of his remaining guards a Gallic mercenary.

> Seeing a certain Bituitus there, leader of the Gauls he said: 'I have gained so much from your right arm against my enemies, now I shall gain most of all if you kill me and save me from the danger of being paraded in a Roman triumph, a man who had been the king of such a great state, but who now cannot die by this poison because fool that he was, he has employed others as antidotes. While I was vigilant against those poisons that can be administered to a man through his food, I forgot about the most deadly poison of them all that exists in the house of every king, the envy of his army, children and friends.' Bituitus was overcome with pity and delivered the death blow as the king wanted.   (App., *Mith.* 16.111)

Pompey received the news in Sinope which was where Pharnaces sent his father's body by ship together with any remaining hostages, and those who had been involved in the murder of M'. Aquillius so many years before.[17] He also asked Pompey if he was to be allowed to rule his paternal kingdom or just the Crimea. Pompey provided suitable funeral rites for Mithridates and the ashes were placed in the royal tomb at Sinope. To Pharnaces he gave the Bosporan kingdom which his brother Machares had ruled except for the town of Phanagoria which he declared a free state. Pharnaces turned out to be a chip off the old block, however, and was evidently not content with a position as an ally of Rome and ruler of a minor state on the periphery of the Hellenistic-Roman World. It appears that he soon extended his rule over Phanagoria, and took full advantage of the later civil war between Caesar and Pompey to take Sinope in 47, although this conquest was not long lasting, and when defeated by Caesar returned to the Crimea where he was killed in fighting for his kingdom about 45. He was the last of his line, and the Bosporus too came under Roman control.

So in the end, Mithridates had done Pompey's job for him, and critics of the latter could say quite justifiably that this general had done little to actually win this campaign, and that Lucullus had done the dirty work for another to gain the benefits and the glory. Lucullus and Pompey were never reconciled. Houseman's poetic pronouncement on Mithridates is perhaps a suitable conclusion to this episode of Roman history.

> There was a king reigned in the East;
> There, where kings will sit to feast,
> They get their fill before they think
> With poisoned meat and poisoned drink.

He gathered all that sprang to birth
From the many-venomed earth;
First a little, thence to more,
He sampled all her killing store;
And easy smiling, seasoned sound
Sate the king when healths went round.
They put arsenic in his meat
And stared aghast to watch him eat;
They poured strychnine in his cup
And shook to see him drink it up;
They shook, they stared as white's their shirt:
Them it was their poison hurt.
... I tell the tale that I heard told.
Mithridates, he died old.

        (A.E. Houseman, *A Shropshire Lad*, LXII)

Chapter 11

The Grand Settlement

He lies below
The shore at Rhoiteion, pinned by that Trojan ground ...
So, brother more dear to me than my own life-breath,
Never, again shall I see you

(Catullus, Poem 69)[1]

It is often assumed that Roman territorial arrangements made in Asia Minor and Syria, and the redrawing of the empire's frontiers occurred subsequent to the death of Mithridates VI. In fact, however, this was an ongoing process which had begun even before Pompey took up his command in 66. During the last phase of Lucullus' command a commission made up of ten senators had already been assigned, as was the normal procedure, to supervise any new acquisitions especially where these were connected with tribute and taxation. As has been pointed out earlier in this discussion, any wars fought by Rome had to be paid for; and any defeated state was expected to finance monetary losses incurred by the victors either in annual tribute or by extraordinary one-off payments. This had obviously been imposed on Antiochus III of Syria and had clearly been decided as a consequence of the massive expenditure Mithridates had caused Rome. This was also to be seen again in the negotiations with Tigranes of Armenia. More than this, however, because of the instability in the northern Levant and Mesopotamia and throughout Asia Minor, the defeat of Mithridates affected the entire region while the capitulation of Tigranes, who had absorbed the remnants of Antiochus III's once-great kingdom, brought much uncertainty to Syria and the regions immediately to the south bordering Ptolemaic Egypt, itself no longer a major force in the eastern Mediterranean.

So Pompey after his largely diplomatic victory over Tigranes had returned Cappadocia to the rule of Ariobarzanes and added to it those lands of Sophene and Gordyene, formerly granted to the younger Tigranes, while Commagene was confirmed as the kingdom of Antiochus. Such grants were of course meant to be ratified by the senate through a decree reached either by consensus or by a majority vote among senators. But such was Pompey's authority based on the powers of his recent and current commands that his *acta* or deeds were unlikely to be challenged at home. There were challenges to aspects of his settlement especially regarding a request for land allocation for an unstipulated number of his veteran soldiers, and delaying tactics were employed by his political enemies, but the bulk of his achievements were accepted without emendation once his new-found political ally Julius Caesar was elected consul for 59.

After founding a city in Lesser Armenia called Nicopolis, at Dasteira most likely the site of his victory over Mithridates in 66, during the course of 64–63 Pompey led his army south into Syria where, to end the chaos caused by Tigranes' conquest of the area and the internecine strife among the previous dynasty, the kingdom was converted into a Roman province. The pleas of its last king Antiochus XIII to be restored to his kingdom were ignored since Pompey considered Syria a Roman prize won from Tigranes of Armenia. While at Antioch he mediated a border dispute between Armenia and Parthia, and may have contemplated a campaign against this Asian power but stopped short of emulating Lucullus and risking a loss of goodwill at Rome. His legate L. Afranius had however already been active against Parthians in an earlier breach of the peace and had penetrated the Tigris valley as far as Arbela (Plut., *Pomp.* 36.2).[2] From Antioch Pompey was drawn south into Coele-Syria, modern Palestine, which had once been the much disputed border between the Seleucids and the Ptolemies. In this area, ancient Israel had again become an independent Jewish state under the rule of the Hasmonaean dynasty since 167 BC when Matthias had led a Jewish rebellion – the insurgents were called the Maccabees – which had defeated Antiochus IV. Subsequently, Simon the Hasmonaean had been proclaimed the first king of Judaea in 140 BC, and when the kingdom achieved recognition by Rome in 139, although its immediate overlord remained the Syrian king. In 64 Judaea was ruled by Aristobulus II but his brother Hyrcanus also sought the throne and a state of civil war between the two allowed the Romans to become involved. In 63 Pompey had reached Jericho, according to the Jewish historian Josephus (*BJ*. 1.138), Petra according to Plutarch (*Pomp.* 41.3), when he heard of the suicide of Mithridates. At this stage, the Roman general was more concerned with the illegal activities of the Nabataean Arabs under their king Aretas whose aggressive attacks had become a cause for concern. In the event, the Nabataeans were sufficiently intimidated to agree to terms, and Pompey instead besieged Jerusalem for three months before it was sacked and Aristobulus captured. Hyrcanus was allowed to become High Priest but not a king and Judaea was from then on to be supervised from Antioch and a future Roman governor.

This brought Pompey's campaigning in the East to a conclusion and with it his geopolitical remapping of the entire region. In Asia Minor the new Roman provinces were Pontus and Bithynia, alongside the existing provinces of Asia (capital at Pergamum) and Cilicia, and now with Syria to the south. But these provinces were to be protected by an intricate framework of client and allied states; from around the Euxine, the Bosporan kingdom and Colchis; in Asia Minor itself, Lesser Armenia, Paphlagonia, Galatia, Cappadocia; further to the south, Commagene, several minor states around Syria and Cilicia, Judaea and Nabataea; to the East, Armenia and Sophene. As Seager points out, there is clear indication of much forethought and planning in the arrangement as they affected Asia Minor but less evidence of a considered approach to the affairs of the states in the Levant.[3]

The settlement engineered by Pompey on behalf of the Roman Empire is often regarded as one which endured for centuries. In general terms this may be an acceptable proposition, although the situation came under severe threat within a decade following Crassus' catastrophic defeat by the Parthians at Carrhae in 53. This debacle, on a par with Cannae and Arausio, might easily have led to the immediate collapse of the Roman Empire in Asia if the vast majority of the client kings and chiefs, installed between 64 and 63 had not remained faithful to their public treaties with Rome and, perhaps more significantly, with their private agreements with Pompey. As it was the new province of Syria must have been sufficiently well garrisoned to withstand a Parthian onslaught, while the military forces of allies such as Deiotarus of Galatia were able to plug any gaps. The Parthians, whose king resented the fact that victory over the Romans had been accomplished by his general Surena not himself, also did not take full advantage of their victory. C. Cassius Longinus, Crassus' quaestor and left in command when Crassus himself was killed at truce negotiations, led 10,000 survivors of an army numbering about 45,000 back into Syria from northern Mesopotamia and continued to lead the defence against Parthian attacks. The Parthian menace on this occasion was thwarted, the eastern frontier of the Roman Empire hardly, however, stabilised. Antioch, one of the Empire's most populous and important cities was to remain vulnerable to attack from the East and a garrison of three legions was to be permanently established in the new province as a bulwark against Parthian hostilities.

Still the settlement of Asia Minor and Syria was seen by later writers as a seminal point in the history of the Roman Empire. Thus the elder Pliny (*NH* 7.99) writing about one hundred years after this event claims that Pompey later said this episode in his career was a particularly gratifying one since he had found 'Asia Minor the furthest of the provinces and made it one in the centre instead.' Meanwhile, the second-century-AD historian Florus (1.40.31) states that:

> Excepting the Parthians who preferred a treaty and the people of India who still are unaware of us, all Asia between the Red and Caspian Seas and the Ocean was now held by us having been

conquered or intimidated into submission by Pompey's campaigns and show of arms.

Appian comments that:

> After forty-two years, the Romans conquered King Mithridates and also subjected to their rule Bithynia, Cappadocia, and other neighbouring states around the Euxine Sea. Since the war with Mithridates had as a consequence seen their rule extended from Spain and the Pillars of Hercules to the Euxine Sea and the desert which borders Egypt and the River Euphrates, it is appropriate that this victory should be called great and that Pompey who led the army should also have acquired the title 'the Great.'
>
> (App., *Mith.* 17.121)

Finally Plutarch in his biography of Pompey says that:

> His triumph was so great that although two days had been allocated for it the time was still insufficient and many of the displays which should have been in the procession found no place and could have adorned another such occasion. Inscriptions carried at the start of the procession referred to the states which he had conquered: Pontus, Armenia, Cappadocia, Paphlagonia, Media, Colchis, Iberia, Albania, Syria, Cilicia, Mesopotamia, Phoenicia, Palestine, Judaea and Arabia and moreover all the power of the pirates in their various strongholds on land or on the sea. (*Pomp.* 45.1–2)

Appendix 1

The Ancient Sources

Any study of a historical subject naturally requires the research to take account of the sources, selecting not only the most dependable and relevant but also the temporal relationship to the events in question and constructing from these as far as possible a fair and accurate picture. This same general rule applies to the study of the wars fought in the eastern Mediterranean in the second and first centuries BC which left Rome with an entirely new empire in Asia Minor and Syria. There is however a peculiar set of problems which affect the historian writing of events in antiquity which is perhaps less in evidence for more modern historical subjects. These particular problems can be itemized as: the length of time elapsing between the events to be studied and their coverage by the ancient writers; the length of time from the events to the present day which may have resulted in changes to the geography, topography even climate over a space of two to three thousand years; the survival of the sources, which may mean that the best has been lost; and the difficulty of revisiting sites including battlefields if sources are vague about their whereabouts – as they often are. For this study the most important ancient writers in chronological order are Polybius, Livy, Plutarch and Appian. Only Livy wrote in Latin.

Polybius (*c*.220–125) is certainly our most important source for the background to Rome's war with Antiochus III and would certainly have been a first-choice source for the entire hostilities had this section of his history survived. Polybius was a Greek from Achaea who served in a senior capacity in the Achaean League in its war with Rome and when it was defeated in 168 became a hostage to ensure his own city's future good behaviour. His time in Rome brought him contact with Scipio Aemilianus, one of the most influential men of his time, and through this connection and perhaps at his prompting he undertook to write a history dealing with the period of Rome's growth from Italian state to world power. Naturally his coverage of the major wars of the period between 264 and 146 was detailed and knowledgeable and if his discussion of particular battles might be considered a little careless or imprecise, for the most part he is sure guide to events. Sadly his work becomes fragmentary after Book 6, therefore the war against Antiochus and Roman dealings with Syria in the second century BC have for the most part been lost.

Livy (59 BC–AD 17) used Polybius as his main source for Roman foreign affairs and is generally faithful to the original. Thus where Polybius breaks off Livy's account may be regarded as being a fair reflection of the source. Nonetheless, Livy has his drawbacks since his knowledge of military matters came second-hand since he did not pursue a public or political career. He clearly does not have a fine appreciation of tactics or logistics when describing campaigns or battles. Still his history is the main source for events in the period 200–168 BC, after which his account is also lost and survives only in brief excerpts called Epitomes.

Plutarch (AD 50–120), philosopher-cum-polymath, wrote among numerous other works a series of parallel lives of famous Greeks and Romans, often chosen for what may seem to us spurious or contrived reasons. These paired biographies are a major source of information for both the Classical period of Greece and the Roman Republic. He has the least to say about the war between the Romans and Antiochus III since any details he possesses emerge only through his life of the elder Cato and this is related primarily to the battle of Thermopylae in 191. A life of Scipio Africanus was probably written but is lost and this would have contained material on the battle of Magnesia-ad-Sipylum. Other major players of this period: Philip V, T. Quinctius Flamininus, Eumenes II of Pergamum or indeed Antiochus himself clearly did not suit his task or he could find no suitable parallels. It is quite the opposite when we come to the war against Mithridates VI of Pontus since there is neither Polybius nor Livy to draw information from. It is true that Livy exists in brief summaries written much later than the original work, and he is an obvious source for the later Roman historians Appian and Orosius, but generally little worthwhile can be reconstructed from the existing summaries. Plutarch by default therefore becomes a major source for the Mithridatic wars here since he is interested in several late Roman Republican figures including Gaius Marius, Lucius Cornelius Sulla, Lucius Licinius Lucullus and Gnaeus Pompeius, all of whom to one extent or another were touched by the events of this time (89–64 BC). Indeed for Lucullus and Pompey this war had far-reaching consequences for both their own careers but also for the progress of the Roman Empire. Plutarch, like many other ancient writers, can be highly useful but also infuriating. First and foremost it is as well to remember that Plutarch is not interested in history per se but in the characters of his subject and how they develop or change according to fate and chance occurrences which affected their lives. Cato's role in the battle of Thermopylae for example, notwith-standing the fact that it derives either from Livy or Cato's own account so one must surely expect a certain bias, is also included to illustrate his competence in *res militaris* or military affairs, and that he excelled the commander Manius Acilius Glabrio, another political newcomer, but that he was humble enough to serve in a minor capacity even though by then an ex-consul. On the other hand, Plutarch's erudition should be ignored at one's peril since he very clearly read widely and had a profound memory for data which he could recollect very probably with commendable accuracy. He was also not unacquainted with battlefields and military campaigns, since he was from an elite family in Boeotia in Greece with friendship ties with senators at Rome, one of whom conducted him around the battlefield at Bedriacum (Cremona). This was where in April 69 the legions supporting Vitellius, the contender for supreme power, defeated those forces supporting the emperor Otho. After the battle Otho committed suicide. When he visited Bedriacum, probably in the 90s, Plutarch was engaged in writing a series of biographies of the Roman emperors. Overall, Plutarch has his limitations, as do all sources, but without his works our knowledge and understanding of Graeco-Roman history would be very poor indeed.

Appian's thematic approach to his subject which is a study of Rome's various and many wars perhaps accounts for its survival since the organisation of the work by geography rather than general chronology makes it highly accessible. It allows the reader or the modern researcher to study individual wars such as those with Carthage, Macedonia, against the Gauls, those in Iberia, the civil wars which afflicted Rome or the wars with Syria, with Mithridates, with Egypt without having breaks in the narrative where other historians such as Polybius or Livy turn to other foreign affairs or domestic issues. Appian (*c*.90–150), an Egyptian Greek and probably a civil servant rather than a military man, clearly spent a good deal of time in his research, but he is clearly not as detailed as Livy would have been where we have this historian's account of the same episodes. And not only is Livy the basic source for much of Appian's material, which shows that the latter read Latin or obtained his information through a translated text, but then he sometimes makes very basic errors and indicates that his interpretation of events may also be flawed. Having said that he is the prime source for the events in the Mithridatic wars and especially for background material dealing with events in Asia Minor in the second half of the second century BC. He preserves something of Livy's coverage, perhaps mostly accurate, although the reader should always be aware that this is not how the original would have been presented.

Besides the four main writers some material for the final war against Mithridates may be found among the speeches of Cicero who actively supported Pompey in his ambition to assume command of the war in place of Lucullus. There is also the work of Memnon of Heracleia in Pontus, who wrote a history of his city probably in the first century AD. The work is partially preserved in the Byzantine collection of Photius, and provides additional and corroborative information found in the main sources. His work may not be particularly elaborate or extensive but he is important as one of the very few non-Roman writers available to us and useful for illustrating a local viewpoint of international affairs.

Moreover, there is inscriptional and numismatic evidence which can sometimes provide additional insight into certain episodes or can illustrate certain extra facets of the situation such as propaganda which appears on the coins of the protagonists. Roman Republican coinage in particular was increasingly used to convey topical information and to celebrate victories or the careers of individuals. It was certainly used in this fashion by both Sulla and Pompey who make references to their campaigns in Asia Minor. Rome's opponents too used the coinage as a medium of propaganda and the coins issued by the Seleucids or by Mithridates allow some clue, however slight, into the psyche of the enemy. The victor writes the history and certainly the extent of Roman successes has meant that very little material exists from the losing side. This too must be considered when writing a history of Rome's wars in the East.

Appendix 2

Chronology of the Mithridatic Wars

Spring 88	Mithridates ordered the invasion of the Roman province of Asia
Spring 87	Sulla arrived in Epirus
March 86	Sulla captured Athens
Summer 86	Battle of Chaeronea and defeat of Archelaus
Summer 86	Lucullus defeated a Pontic fleet at Tenedos
Summer 85	Defeat of Archelaus and Taxiles at Orchomenus
Summer 85	Fimbria defeated Mithridates at the Rhyndacus river
Summer 85	Treaty of Dardanus
83–81	'The Adventure of Murena' – the second war with Mithridates
74	Mithridates' attack on Bithynia and the assault on Chalcedon
Spring 73	Arrival of Lucullus in Asia
73	Mithridates moved to besiege Cyzicus
Winter 73	The siege of Cyzicus broken
72	Mithridates retreated to Pontus followed by Lucullus
Summer 69	Lucullus invaded Armenia
October 69	Battle at Tigranocerta
68	Lucullus marched towards Artaxata. Battle at the River Arsanias
Winter 68/7	Lucullus at Nisibis
67	Pompey took command of the campaign
Winter 66/5	Mithridates at Dioscurias
63	Suicide of Mithridates
64–63	Eastern Settlement of Pompey
61	Pompey's triumph in Rome

Notes

Chapter 1 (pp. 1–6)

1. The excavation of 'tophets' on a number of Punic sites have been identified as areas associated with the sacrifice of the 'first born', not uniquely Punic but certainly most openly practised by these people. See, for example, on the Punic site of Motya in western Sicily.

2. *Provincia* is really the title of an area of command for a Roman official. Thus Italy could be as much a province of the empire as a region overseas.

3. Polybius actually starts his coverage of Roman history with the beginning of the First Punic War (264) probably taking up the history of Rome and especially Sicily from the conclusion of a history by Timaeus of Tauromenion. Polybius also concluded his work not in 167 but in 146, at least and probably later still. He was present at the destruction of Carthage and lived into the 120s spending most of his time in Rome, although by birth a Greek from Achaea in the Peloponnese.

4. T.P. Wiseman, *The Myths of Rome* (Exeter 2004) 53–4, 66. The earliest connections with Greece, specifically Delphi and Athens, are dated to the late sixth and mid-fifth centuries respectively. These may well be the inventions of later Roman writers and preserved in the history of Livy which refers to these events. However, these tales may also reflect a memory of contacts with Greek states and so contain an element of truth.

5. For Roman diplomacy and campaigns in Illyria between 230 and 219, see R.M. Errington, 'Rome and Greece to 205 B.C.', *The Cambridge Ancient History*, Second Edition (Cambridge 1989) Volume 8, 85–94. The Romans twice committed armies of about 20,000 to the region to ensure peace on their eastern seaboard, and seem to have established a permanent presence at Pharos and had contacts with the Greeks on the mainland, not to mention expelling Illyrian invaders from Corcyra.

6. Sabin, P., *Lost Battles: Reconstructing the Great Clashes of the Ancient World* (London 2007) 579–80.

7. For a discussion of this point, see A. Lampela, *Rome and the Ptolemies of Egypt* (Helsinki 1998) 41.

8. The Romans used base metals as currency probably by the end of the fourth century. The circulation of silver and later gold coins, initially minted and designed by Greek craftsmen from Campania, probably

Neapolis, was late compared to the Greek cities of Sicily and Magna
Graecia (southern Italy) which had been coining since about 500 BC.

9. Lampela (1998) 33, and n. 29 for the ancient sources; J.D. Grainger,
The Roman War of Antiochos the Great (Leiden 2002) 5–8; W.V. Harris,
War and Imperialism in Republican Rome 327–70 BC (Oxford 1992) 183–4;
T.R.S. Broughton, *The Magistrates of the Roman Republic* (New York
1951–52) Vol. 1, 197. It is claimed that Ptolemy II Philadelphus initiated
the treaty by sending an embassy, an act which was reciprocated; and it
was the Romans who took full advantage of having a friendly and 'neutral'
Egypt in the First Punic War (264–241). Thereafter, the contacts may
have 'remained loose and remote,' as Lampela claims (1998) 91, but they
certainly remained.

10. Lampela (1998) 60–2.

11. Hence the myth of M. Aemilius Lepidus' (cos. 178) tutorship of the new
king and denarii proclaiming this connection issued by the later triumvir
Lepidus in about 58 BC, R.J. Evans, 'The Moneyership of Marcus
Lepidus Triumvir', *Acta Classica* 33 (1990) 103–4. A real tutorship in
effect regency from a distance would certainly have illustrated Egypt's loss
of status, but there is no ancient evidence for this smart piece of family
propaganda. Cf. R.D. Weigel, *Lepidus: the Tarnished Triumvir* (London
1992) 8, who considers the episode historical. Moreover, E.S. Gruen's
argument, *The Hellenistic World and the Coming of Rome* (Berkeley 1986)
680–2, that this was too early a date for such an approach by the Romans is
perhaps too cautious. The Romans knew well enough the importance of
controlling another state, but at that stage there was no need for such
control.

12. For the date of the embassy see Broughton (1951–52) 1.321–328.

13. For the work and mission of the embassy consisting of the ex-consuls
C. Claudius Nero and P. Sempronius Tuditanus and the much younger
M. Aemilius Lepidus, see H.H. Scullard, *Roman Politics 200–150 B.C.*
(Oxford 1973) 94; Lampela (1998) 76–97.

14. Broughton (1951–52) 1.321 and n. 4.

15. See Errington (1998) 83 and n. 4 for the ancient sources.

16. This came about as a result of the Roman war with the Illyrians, M.H.
Crawford, *The Roman Republic* (London 1978) 63. 'Friends' of Rome
might be a more accurate description, Gruen (1986) 55–8.

17. The refounding of Hipponion in *c.*379/8, which had been destroyed by
Dionysius, tyrant of Syracuse, a decade before, shows that Roman influence at that stage did not extend to the far south of the Italian peninsula,
Diodorus, 15.24.1. This event must also throw considerable doubt on
the treaties supposedly signed between Rome and Carthage delineating

specific spheres of influence as early as 509 according to Polybius, 3.22.1–26.1; N. Lewis & M. Reinhold, *Roman Civilisation: Sourcebook I: The Republic* (Columbia 1966) 70–3.
18. On Rome and Troy see A. Erskine, *Rome and Troy* (Oxford 2000) 15.
19. Crawford (1978) 63.
20. Syracuse in particular had assumed this role for many years between about 480 and 275 BC, but Tarentum (the Greek colony of Taras) had also been active in the region.

Chapter 2 (pp. 7–18)

1. The translation here is adapted from that of the *Loeb Classical Library Edition*. All other translations herein are similarly adapted or my own.
2. On the authenticity of this evidence, Grainger (2002) 10–12; Lampela (1998) 248–9; Gruen (1986) 64–5.
3. On the difficulties of the text which contains an Antiochus as the Syrian king, see Lampela (1998) 52–53.
4. A.B. Bosworth, *The Legacy of Alexander: Politics, Warfare, and Propaganda under the Successors* (Oxford 2002) 210.
5. Antigonus, as his name suggests, was the son of Demetrius Poliorcetes, grandson of Antigonus Monophthalmos. The family ruled Macedonia down to the deposition of Perseus, its last king, in 168.
6. Ceraunus was a son of Ptolemy Lagus, half-brother to Ptolemy II and probably older but excluded from power. In exile at the court of Seleucus he became close to the king but plotted against him in order to make his own attempt at winning Macedonia. He was killed fighting Gallic tribes in the Balkans in 279.
7. For the difficulties about the precise date see H. Sidky, *The Greek Kingdom of Bactria* (New York 2000) 138–52.
8. Sidky (2000) 227–8.
9. Possibly down to about 55 BC, as suggested by A.K. Narain, 'The Greeks of Bactria and India' in *The Cambridge Ancient History*, Volume 8, Second Edition (Cambridge 1989) 412–21.
10. See further in Chapter 5 Note 8 and Chapter 11.
11. It is notable that Cleopatra VII the last Ptolemaic queen of Egypt, who committed suicide in 30 BC, was unique among her family dynasty in being able to understand and speak the language of her subjects.
12. It is very noticeable that with the exception of the first two Seleucids, the Syrian kings died young, rarely more than fifty years of age, often in their twenties and thirties, which meant that rulers came to the throne as minors, another sure recipe for instability. However, they were clearly also

energetic and warlike in keeping with their Macedonian and warrior heritage, and several died in military engagements.

13. Ptolemy's victory in battle may not have been that decisive or the battle may have incurred high casualties on the Egyptian side. His willingness to reach a peace not particularly beneficial to him is rather telling.

14. E.R. Bevan, *The House of Seleucus* (London 1902) Volume 1, 193–4; see further below in Chapter 4.

15. A daughter named Laodice is noted by Polybius, 5.74.4, 8.22.11.

16. It is one of those paradoxes of history that many of the best remembered and esteemed generals in history were in fact not ultimately victors such as Hannibal, Pompey, Napoleon, and Rommel. Scipio Africanus, Caesar, Wellington and Montgomery are perhaps less esteemed yet were the ultimate conquerors. Antiochus does not appear to have been the subject of a biography in antiquity and only features prominently in the histories of Polybius, Livy and Appian as an enemy of Rome.

17. It is extraordinary that the capital of the Seleucid kingdom lay so close to hostile territory and that its own port was in enemy hands. The frontier with Egypt was a mere few miles to the south. It does, however, indicate that for most of the time the two kingdoms maintained a peace which was probably economically beneficial to both.

18. Polybius (5.79.2) tells us that Ptolemy had 73 elephants, 40 on the left wing, 33 on the right, while Antiochus had 60 on his right wing, and 42 on his right wing, a total of 102 (5.79.13).

19. Polybius is clearly ill informed here and perhaps did not have much acquaintance with the use of elephants in combat. These had been used extensively in battles by the Greeks since the reign of Alexander the Great. Something else must have disturbed the Ptolemaic elephants or they were simply not as well trained.

20. Polybius does not tell us whether or not Antiochus was obliged to surrender all his very recent acquisitions including Seleucia. If he was forced to give up this last city it would have been humiliating and meant that an Egyptian garrison was again installed almost within a stone's throw of the walls of his capital. It should probably be assumed that Seleucia was now permanently in Syrian hands.

21. On the size of Antiochus' army, see Grainger (2002) 271 & 316. For the significance of Raphia, see Lampela (1998) 241: 'The Ptolemaic army won its last great victory in the battle of Raphia in 217.'

22. Early May is probably meant here.

23. The citadel at Sardis was notoriously difficult to assault. The Greeks had failed on more than one occasion before, for example, in the Ionian revolt

in 499 when it was held by the satrap Artaphermes while the city itself was torched.

24. Polybius also adds a moralistic note, 8.36.8–9, that the manner of Achaeus' capture and demise brought him sympathy and contempt and hatred for those who had organised and carried out the plan.

25. The fate of Achaeus' wife Laodice goes unrecorded, but by her name also related to the royal family. In normal circumstances the fate of the head of the immediate family would have been visited on the other members. Perhaps if her involvement was passive she was lucky.

26. For the ambitions of Attalus see the next chapter.

27. The court apparently contrived to keep the death of the monarch secret for about a year in order it is claimed for the king's immediate circle to ransack the palace in Alexandria and make their fortunes.

28. Antiochus did indeed have two sons both of whom took the name of their father but his third son who became Antiochus IV in 175, only acquired the name after the death of his older brother in 193. Antiochus second son was named Seleucus who became king in 187. It is just conceivable that all three sons were present at Panion but it is more likely that at least one was left to supervise the kingdom in the king's absence.

Chapter 3 (pp. 19–24)

1. The first century writer Strabo divides Asia into the lands west and north of the Taurus Mountains, including modern Ukraine and Russia, and those to the south including India and Persia. Books 11–14 cover the former, Book 15 the latter.

2. It is worth pointing out that these lesser states in Asia Minor did not always rush to obey the commands of Rome even when the Romans were quite clearly the dominant power in the Mediterranean. Inter-state relations continued in very much the same way they had operated for centuries.

3. Appian adds the interesting note (*Mith.* 1.4) that the indemnity was actually less than the plunder Prusias had obtained.

4. Appian retells an amusing story, probably from Livy either ultimately derived from Valerius Antias or the elder Cato from whose 'authentic sayings' this statement is said to belong. The urban praetor charged with sending an embassy delayed since he personally favoured Nicomedes, but finally selected three senators, one of whom had recently been hit on the head by a stone, one who had gout and one who was regarded as plain stupid. Cato is supposed to have said that this embassy had 'no sense, no feet and no head' (*Mith.* 1.6). For the senators concerned see Broughton (1951) 1.460, M. Licinius, A. Hostilius Mancinus, L. Manlius Vulso.

5. Nicomedes IV, grandson of this Nicomedes, bequeathed his kingdom to the Romans in 75/4.
6. Hellenistic kingships proliferate after Ipsus in 302/1 as several of the former generals of Alexander started to style themselves as kings. Others such as Agathocles, the tyrant of Syracuse, soon followed suit. Therefore, it is perhaps likely that Eumenes was in fact a 'king' from rather earlier in his rule than is generally supposed. There is absolutely no reason for Pergamum to buck such an attractive trend.
7. For a discussion of the law and its possible date see R.J. Evans, *Gaius Marius: A Political Biography* (Pretoria 1994) 195–6.

Chapter 4 (pp. 25–46)

1. On this treaty see most recently the cogent arguments of Ekstein (2008) 121–80.
2. Not all were ships of war since there must have been a large number of transport ships for the infantry, horses, and other equipment and logistical supplies all defended by a strong detachment of warships of various forms from trireme to quinquereme.
3. Appian, *Syr.* 2.7–8, says that Hannibal had previously urged the king to give him an army of 10,000 with which to invade Italy and promised aid from Carthage. This may be pure invention from a source hostile to Hannibal. In any case, neither situation occurred.
4. See Grainger (2002) 316–17, for a discussion of the size of the army which, based on that available for Raphia and Panion, he estimates that some 20,000 potential troops were left in readiness in the south in case of any incursion from Egypt should Ptolemy or rather his advisers decide to take a more proactive and pro-Roman stance.
5. They had already switched allegiance to and from the Romans more than once in the previous twenty years. Any seasoned diplomat would have been wary of any promises given out by representatives of the Aetolian League.
6. It is curious that Hannibal who also features in this war is said to have failed in his invasion of Italy mainly because of a lack of siege equipment yet he cannot have lacked the current technology nor the resources to provide his army which siege specialists and their equipment. Others like Antiochus travelling light could do this. Perhaps Hannibal unwisely chose to ignore this arm of his military capability and with initial successes such as the rebellions against Rome of cities such as Tarentum, Capua and Syracuse he was rather careless about this issue, which rather puts a dent in his otherwise famous reputation.

7. Appian, *Syr.* 3.16, says that Philip was in two minds about his treaty with Rome. When Antiochus came upon the unburied dead of Cynoscephalae he saw to the burial rites of those who had laid where they had fallen five years before in the hope that these religious observances would cause the Macedonians to rid themselves of their king who had not fulfilled this obligation. He was again wrong in his assumption.
8. M. Baebius Tamphilus was praetor in 191 and clearly in some roving command. Ap. Claudius Pulcher (consul in 185) must have been a legate rather than quaestor in 190. Broughton, *Magistrates of the Roman Republic* 1.353, 355.
9. Appian, *Syr.* 4.17, puts Antiochus' army at 10,000 foot and 500 horse prior to the battle of Thermopylae which may indicate that his invasion force was originally somewhat higher, but precision is impossible here since the numbers credited to his allies, few though these were, are not given.
10. Appian adds that Antiochus' defence involved the use of siege engines, presumably catapults which he had brought with him.
11. Appian also says that the main Aetolian force never engaged at all but remained encamped at Heracleia, a decidedly lukewarm commitment from such previously belligerent allies.
12. Plutarch's lack of enthusiasm for Cato is quite evident but forthright too since this engagement was a minor affair in comparison with what was to come in this war.
13. Appian refers to presumably this same Polyxenidas as the commander in overall charge of the Seleucid army which Antiochus had summoned. He was clearly trusted and held a very senior position, which illustrates the importance at this stage that Antiochus placed on the naval arm of his defence of Asia Minor.
14. Appian, *Syr.* 5.22, differentiates between 'decked ships' of which Salinator had eighty-one and Eumenes twenty-five, and undecked ships of which there were twenty-five Pergamene. The decked ships were probably quinqueremes while the undecked smaller vessels like the trireme or bireme.
15. The senate, as a collective body of government, seems to have been intent on appointing one of the two new consuls each year as supreme commander in this campaign against Antiochus, and not as had sometimes been the case in previous wars where a consul had had his command prorogued as proconsul, for example, Scipio Africanus in Iberia and Quinctius Flamininus against Philip V. This indicates two things, either that the senate did not regard Antiochus as a very great threat to Roman power or more likely that the body as whole was concerned that individual senators should not make too much capital out of a victory, and that any victory or conceivably any defeat would be a collective one. Hence Glabrio had been

commander from the spring of 191 until relieved in the spring of 190, the Scipios hoped to complete their work by the spring of 189, which they did.

16. The senate had authorised the Scipios, in the event of the king showing true goodwill to the Roman cause, to relieve him of his war indemnity, App., *Syr.* 5.23.

17. Notable ancient naval battles that actually took place on land include Aegospotami in 405, between the Athenians and Sparta, Eurymedon in 456 between Athens and the Persians, the battle of Actium in 31 BC was more on land than on sea, even the battle of Salamis in 480 between the Greeks and Persians had episodes on the land as well as on the sea.

18. This would be the end of the sailing season in 190 probably late September early October and the onset of winter storms.

19. The recent arrival of the praetor Regillus must indicate a date in the spring of 190, Salinator having returned to Rome in the winter of 191/0.

20. Appian's figures, *Syr.* 5.27, show that a large element of the Roman fleet was engaged elsewhere possibly shadowing the advance of the army in Thrace and that the Pergamene detachment was at its base in Elaia, but also that the Seleucid fleet had been substantially upgraded during the previous winter.

21. Appian, *Syr.* 5.27, says twenty-nine losses from the Seleucid fleet, thirteen captured with crews, Polyxenidas towed the single Rhodian warship into Ephesus.

22. The Rhodians had also maintained their blockade of Hannibal and his fleet in Pamphylia so that he played no further role in the subsequent events.

23. The susceptibility of commanders, perhaps not yet specifically Roman, to accept bribes was clearly a commonplace. We are not told if the Scipios succumbed, but there were later suspicions that Africanus had been bribed by Antiochus and the attacks to which he was subjected and court action forced him into premature retirement and death at just fifty-five. Appian's account at this juncture, *Syr.* 6.29, digresses to give a lengthy account of the captured young Scipio, about whom he was clearly confused. Africanus' son did not have an illustrious career, but he did adopt a son of L. Aemilius Paullus, the victor over Perseus of Macedonia at Pydna in 168, who became Scipio Aemilianus, the conqueror of Carthage, hence the second Africanus. Africanus' son was returned shortly after the conclusion of these talks.

24. Was this because Antiochus felt that Africanus would be more sympathetic in victory or that a battle led, in effect, by the conqueror of Hannibal would be a special conflict in the minds of men? Ever conscious of one's place in history and in the histories written by court historians, victory over an army led by the famous Africanus would indeed be glorious, but

defeat also less of a disgrace. It may be too that Africanus' 'illness' was politically motivated to avoid being on the field of an enemy whose bribes may have compromised the Roman. Appian does say that Africanus specifically advised the king to wait for his return, *Syr.* 6.30.

25. Ahenobarbus was clearly a senior member of the consul's staff since he had been himself consul the year before. He was the direct ancestor of the emperor Nero and, like the elder Cato, the first of his family to hold high public office.
26. On the battle at Magnesia see Sabin (2007) 197–200 on the sources: Livy, 37.38–44; App., *Syr.* 6.30–6.
27. Appian, *Syr.* 6.31, says that although the Romans had some elephants these were not considered large enough or in sufficient numbers to be worth employing and were stationed somewhere in the rear of the line of battle.
28. Sabin (2007, 31) says that Livy (37.40) and Appian (*Syr.* 6.32) 'claim that the Seleucid phalangites … at Magnesia deployed no less than 32 deep.'
29. The River Phrygius ran to the right of the right wing commanded by Antiochus, the centre may then have been deployed on sloping ground or even confined by a tributary stream of the river. It is impossible to re-capture the ancient positions since the land today is intensively farmed.
30. Appian, *Syr.* 6.33, adds that Antiochus had what appeared to be two armies, one to attack and another in reserve, and that these were displayed in such a way as to strike terror into the enemy. It seems as if the Syrian monarch held a large number of troops in reserve but more likely because they were simply citizen militia drawn from the levies of numerous cities around his empire and not that well trained.

Chapter 5 (pp. 47–52)

1. Livy places ratification of the treaty in the senate under his account of 190 although it is more likely that, given the date of the battle and the consequent difficulty of travelling to and from Rome in the winter months, the proceedings actually took place in the spring of 189 at the earliest, Livy 37.55–6.
2. Grainger (2002) 356. S. Sherwin-White & A. Kuhrt, *From Samarkand to Sardis* (London 1993) 216 stress that the presence of the Seleucid monarch in Babylon in 188/7 illustrates his continuing domination of the kingdom's internal affairs.
3. This was June or July of 193, Livy 35.15.2, Grainger (2002) 157.
4. His sister Cleopatra (I) had become the wife of Ptolemy V Epiphanes (206/5–180) and regent for their son Ptolemy VI Philometor until her death in 176. Antiochus and Ptolemy were therefore uncle and nephew

respectively. Philometor was detained by his uncle at Memphis but his sister Cleopatra II and younger brother who eventually became Ptolemy VIII Euergetes II (145–116) were proclaimed joint regents in Alexandria.

5. Popillius Laenas had been consul in 172. Noted says Livy for his harsh temper, he had been sent by the senate to prevent a further war between Egypt and Syria. The other envoys were Gaius Hostilius (praetor 170) and Gaius Decimius (praetor 169), H.H. Scullard, *Roman Politics 220–150 B.C.* (Oxford 1973) 210–11.

6. Scullard (1973) 211.

7. The Romans usually sent three-man delegations on foreign business. Cn. Octavius was consul in 165 his colleagues were Sp. Lucretius (pr. 172) and L. Aurelius a probable ex-aedile.

8. The last Seleucid king of any ability was Antiochus VII Sidetes (138–129) who was killed in a battle against the Parthians who, as a result, occupied Mesopotamia which was permanently lost to the Seleucids.

9. C. Habicht, 'The Seleucids and their Rivals', in *The Cambridge Ancient History* (Cambridge 1989) Volume 8. 335. Control of Lycia was however never more than nominal and after 164 the Lycians became self-governing.

10. Publius Scipio Aemilianus, the son of L. Aemilius Paullus victor over Perseus in 168, visited Pergamum probably between 142 and 139, Habicht (1989) 376, as the leading figure in yet another senatorial delegation to the East.

11. Attalus II had founded new cities called Attaleia in Pamphylia and Philadelphia in Lydia, Strabo, 14.4.1, 13.4.10.

12. Aristonicus claimed to be a bastard of Eumenes II, Habicht (1989) 178.

13. Crassus Mucianus had been a supporter of Ti. Gracchus in 133, and was one of the three commissioners dealing with the land allocation. Moreover, he was *pontifex maximus* and his insistence in taking up this command when the chief priest usually remained in Italy had itself caused uproar among political circles.

14. He was captured at Stratoniceia-on-Caicus which suggests that his base was never far from the city of Pergamum which is situated in the same valley. For the city, see T.R.S. Broughton, 'Stratoniceia and Aristonicus', *CP* 29 (1934) 252–4. Aristonicus was later executed in Rome after Aquillius' triumph in 126.

15. Without a regular flow of tribute the allocation of land cannot have had that much impact on the current conditions in Rome, and the work of the commission stalled and was finally abandoned in about 111.

16. Antonius was the grandfather of the more famous Marc Antony, consul in 44 with Julius Caesar.

17. For Cilicia's formal adoption as a province see Evans (1994) 111–15. That this region was not classed as a 'normal' province is easily shown since no senatorial commission was despatched to assess the annual tribute. This only occurred in 64 when Cilicia became a part of the new provincial scheme devised by Pompey for the whole of Asia Minor and Syria. See the final chapter here.

Chapter 6 (pp. 53–63)

1. On the strengths and weakness of Plutarch as a source see Appendix 1.
2. By their oriental not Greek names these officers were probably eunuchs much employed by Mithridates not merely in the palace but also in military functions.
3. Appian says (*Mith.* 3.21) that the king first humiliated this ex-consul then had molten gold poured down his throat as a penalty for Roman avarice. The story appears nowhere else and may be unhistorical but the sort of appropriate death – hubris meeting nemesis.
4. Memnon 22.6 our earliest extant source from the first century AD specifically notes 80,000 deaths, but the epitome of Livy, *Per.* 78, only has 'whomsoever of the Roman citizens was in Asia was killed on one day'; the original may possibly have contained a figure. Our main source Appian (*Mith.* 4.22–3) notes that the king wrote to his governors and others in power locally instructing them to kill 'all Romans and Italians' on the thirtieth day following receipt of his order. Dio 31.101.1, our latest source simply states: 'The people of Asia killed all the Romans on the order of Mithridates.' Memnon, writing in Pontic Heracleia, probably did not employ Livy as a source, but more likely a local historian who may well have exaggerated the total number of deaths to add drama to the episode. Thus while the total number of deaths remains conjectural Roman reaction suggests that something on a great magnitude did take place.
5. Campanian resistance had initially centred on Pompeii, but the rebels had been forced to withdraw from this town to nearby Nola.
6. We do not know the circumstances of the assignment of commands to the consuls of 88. Q. Pompeius Rufus Sulla's colleague and connected through the marriage of Rufus' son to Sulla's daughter, had probably agreed to the Mithridatic command going to Sulla, a general with a secure reputation. But assignment by lot might have been employed as had usually been the case prior to the law of Gaius Gracchus (123–122) which stipulated that consular commands were to be published before the elections were convened.
7. Refusing to march alongside Sulla does not mean that they wished him to fail. Sulpicius and Marius had indulged in a conspiracy, and the consul's

reaction was to fight this sedition with pro-active measures to restore his authority.

8. About 25,000 infantry, not to mention any cavalry units.

9. The *fasces* were bundles of rods carried by a magistrate's guard, the lictors, to illustrate the power to inflict corporal (beating) and capital punishment (decapitation) on citizens. The consul and praetors as senior magistrates wore purple-bordered togas.

10. Plutarch provides the names L. (Minucius) Basilus and C. Mummius as those in charge of this rather vague operation. The names suggest a senatorial or at least an equestrian background. The gate was probably opened by a sympathizer of the consul.

11. Sentius had held this position since 94, Sura was his second-in-command. Achaea was the province which at that stage comprised the whole of Greece and Macedonia.

12. In the fifth century Themistocles had first advocated the joining of the city and its harbour at the Piraeus by a fortification and this had been strengthened and doubled by Pericles later. The city became almost impregnable although the Spartans besieged and forced its capitulation in 404. After this the 'Long Walls' were partly dismantled, but rebuilt in 394 though with Athens' diminished power the walls were not maintained.

13. Sulla's minting of gold coinage in his campaigning in Greece is quite telling since high denomination coins usually indicate specific payments in this case for a fleet to combat that of Mithridates and for the soldiers in his own legions.

14. Plutarch a Boeotian Greek from Chaeronea wrote in the early second century AD and partly used Sulla's own memoirs as a source for this biography, *Sull.* 14.6, but clearly still harboured resentment at Sulla's actions in the war, especially his siege and sack of Athens in 86.

15. Plutarch says that he was poisoned towards the end of the war in 85, *Sull.* 23.2.

16. Plutarch, *Sull.* 15.1, says that Archelaus was stationed off Munychia close to the Piraeus.

17. Hortensius, consul in 69, was later in his career one of the leading Roman orators of the day.

18. Plutarch may have changed sources here using an Athenian writer for the siege of that city plus obvious references to Sulla's own work, then moving to another writer for coverage of the campaign in Boeotia. Compare this with the account of Appian drawing on Livy's history.

19. In his campaign against the Germanic tribes in 104/101 Marius had done precisely the same sort of thing with his men (Plut., *Mar.* 13.1–14.2) – Sulla had been a staff officer there too – though that was caused more by

boredom and a lack of enemy. Sulla either remembered this trick or Plutarch has reused some material here.

20. Some significant similarities with the report of the battle of Thermopylae in 191 are evident. Plutarch says that 3,000 enemy were killed.

21. Plutarch is very vague here since Sulla is unlikely to have treated a loyal city in such a negative way. The Thebans had probably given support to Archelaus and the Pontic army though it is not mentioned by the biographer.

22. Plutarch, *Sull.* 20.4–5, waxes eloquent on the subject of the Plain of Orchomenus and the River Melas, a river which joins the Cephisus which flows near Chaeronea, places all well known to the author.

23. This account clearly comes from Sulla's own account of this battle.

24. For the events unfolding in Rome and Italy at this time see Plutarch, *Sull.* 22.1. Sulla's entourage was increasingly augmented by new exiles from prominent senatorial families who were at odds with the government at Rome.

Chapter 7 (pp. 65–70)

1. Murena may have been a praetor in 88 or elected in 87 and joined Sulla during the course of that troubled year. It is equally possible that he was simply an appointee of Sulla's without Roman magisterial rank and therefore a legate rather than proconsul. His official title may then have been *legatus pro consule* but it is not attested. See Broughton (1952) 2.50 for his possible rank. Murena's son, the consul of 62, and Cicero's client, served under Lucullus. Plutarch, *Luc.* 19.7, has little that is positive to say about this character.

2. Fimbria's suicide is a slightly odd episode which is open to various interpretations. His murder of a consul connected to Cinna and Marius might not have been regarded as sufficient a crime to warrant punishment by Sulla who obviously needed all the support he could garner. Yet there seems to be some considerable animosity between these two men (Plut., *Sull.* 25), which may date back to the time when Fimbria's father was consul with Marius in 104 and when Sulla was a legate in Marius' army.

3. The unstable 80s were followed by the campaigns of Lucullus and Pompey against Mithridates (see below) during which time the Asia Minor cities were called upon to provide financial aid and physical help in food or troops. The end of that conflict brought only a brief respite before the civil wars on the 40s and 30s, between Caesar and Pompey and then Octavian and Antony against Brutus and Cassius, and ultimately Octavian against Antony and Cleopatra, brought many cities to financial ruin. It was only after Octavian's triumph at Actium in 31 and his subsequent long sole rule

of the Roman empire with its concomitant peace that wealth returned to Asia Minor as is seen from the great upsurge in the construction of public buildings which date from the first century AD and afterwards.

4. This was a huge addition to Sulla's personal fortune since the fine did not go to the senate at Rome with which he was at odds. These fines helped finance Sulla's return to Italy and his successful bid for power in 82. His own property and any others assets had been seized when he was declared a public enemy in 87/6.

5. Fifteen years later the Romans were forced to act when piracy had become such a menace that Rome's own port at Ostia had been attacked. With the possibility of famine caused by the disruption to shipping and vital grain imports the people appointed Pompey to free the Mediterranean of pirates, a task he completed in just three months and was rewarded for his efforts by the command against Mithridates. See further below.

6. Broughton (1952) 2.64 leaves the question of the legality of his governorship of Asia unanswered.

7. He did so in 81, Broughton (1952) 77.

8. The son also named Mithridates was suspected by his father of plotting against him and so was lured into a trap, captured and executed, App., *Mith.* 9.64.

9. Pergamum was the chief city of the province of Asia, but Sardis formerly the chief city of Lydia could also have been a good base from which to strike across the mountains into Pontus.

10. Appian, *Mith.* 9.65, states that a private conversation took place. Of course there can have been no contemporary record of this episode and is perhaps what later writers assumed must have happened because of later events. It is certainly the case that in 82 the senate could not have ratified much business such was the state of anarchy in Italy. Murena's position was moreover hardly exceptional at this time.

11. If Murena's retreat was in fact into Phrygia this suggests that the actual fighting took place in Cappadocia and that the Romans were caught when they were again advancing out of the province of Asia in the spring of 81.

12. *Dictator rei publicae constituendae causa*, appointed in November 82 in the absence of the two consuls: the younger Gaius Marius, besieged at Praeneste, and Cn. Papirius Carbo, a fugitive after defeat in battle by the young Pompey. Sulla remained dictator in 81 even when two consuls took office, but almost certainly laid down these powers at the end of that year as he became consul for a second time in 80. His colleague in 80 was Q. Caecilius Metellus Pius, later general against Sertorius in Spain.

13. Since Murena was Sulla's appointee not of the senate, he could also have been relieved of his duties by Sulla. This is possibly implicit in the new prominence given to Gabinius in Appian's account.

14. On the Second Mithridatic War see A. Keaveny, 'Studies in the *Dominatio Sullae*', *Klio* 65 (1983), 185–7. Because Mithridates refused to carry out the full terms of the agreement by handing over the whole of Cappadocia, Sulla refused to ratify the Dardanus agreement. By the time Mithridates fully complied and sent a further legation to Rome to confirm the treaty Sulla had died and the senate, by then dealing with another local crisis in the putsch of the consul M. Aemilius Lepidus, left matters in abeyance. For the time being the affair was left in the air.

Chapter 8 (pp. 71–83)

1. It was a troublesome area only finally cleared of its pirates in 67 by Pompey, although the problem as a whole was not fully solved until the rule of Augustus.

2. It is inevitable that some note of scepticism should be sounded here. It is not impossible that Armenian troops rounded up civilians who would, in such cases, be sold into slavery. It is clear from the ancient sources that much of Anatolia, that part of Asia Minor, away from the coastal belt and the Hellenized urban communities, was rural in character but with quite a dense population, much as today. It is therefore not impossible that Appian gives credible figures although on balance the numbers involved in this transfer of 'free citizens' was probably much less in total.

3. For a detailed discussion see Evans (2003) 133–59.

4. Perperna's official position is not divulged by the sources. He may have been Lepidus' quaestor and, therefore, the official second in command, but in those particular circumstances, a junior official might not have been acceptable to the troops, and he may have in fact been a senior legate, an unofficial position among the general's entourage. He may have been a son of the consul of 92, also M. Perperna, an uncommon name of perhaps Etruscan origin.

5. The Iberian Peninsula from 197 BC was divided by the Romans into the provinces of Near (Citerior) Spain and Far (Ulterior) Spain. Much of what is now Portugal and the Basque country remained unconquered down to the rule of Augustus in the 20s, who then reorganized the region into three provinces: Tarraconensis, Lusitania and Baetica.

6. Both men have names which link them to senatorial families. Magius may indeed have been a junior official in the 80s, while Fannius is probably descended from the consul of 156 and praetor of 118, Broughton (1952) 2.564–5, 584.

7. Plutarch in his biography of Lucullus, 8.5, names only a 'Marius' described as 'one-eyed', 12.5, but this is clearly a case of lapse of memory for M. Varius. Livy's history is likely to have been the ultimate source for both Appian and Plutarch although the latter also mentions Sallust's history which covered the 70s, *Luc.* 11.4.

8. M. Aurelius Cotta had been assigned the new province of Bithynia, Plut., *Luc.* 8.1, Broughton (1952) 2.101 On his death Nicomedes IV (94–75/4), following the example of Attalus III of Pergamum, bequeathed his kingdom to Rome.

9. Plutarch's figure of 120,000 infantry, 16,000 cavalry and 100 scythed chariots (*Luc.* 7.4) is very close to Appian's total, but the latter is more interested in the discrete origins of the forces than in their training.

10. Plutarch, *Luc.* 7.1, notes three legions, but Appian claims five (*Mith.* 11.72) with a total strength of 30,000 infantry and 1,600 cavalry, which if correct perhaps contained levies from the province of Asia. An independent Pergamum had certainly provided troops for Roman armies, while Rhodian vessels were regularly employed in the Roman naval arm.

11. Appian, *Mith.* 10.71, gives a total of 3,000 Roman dead, including one Roman senator L. Manlius.

12. Plutarch, *Luc.* 8.2, says that Cotta lost sixty ships and overall 4,000 men in his defeat at the hands of Mithridates. He also believes that Lucullus was close by Chalcedon, which seems unlikely, and that Mithridates moved his army overland to Cyzicus. Neither Appian nor Plutarch show any interest in being accurate in their geography of the region about which they and probably their sources cannot have been ignorant.

13. The siege of Tyre is related by Diodorus and Arrian in their accounts of Alexander's campaigns, the siege of Syracuse, an important episode in the Second Punic War is recounted by Polybius, Diodorus and Livy. Plutarch in his lives of Alexander and Marcellus also notes certain points. Both sieges are well documented in the literary evidence.

14. Again like Tyre today Bandirma is a peninsula, no longer an island.

15. Appian says that Lucullus had to pass through the lines of Mithridates and that he was aided in this strategy with the connivance of Magius, the Roman rebel, who perhaps hoped for lenient treatment if captured, *Mith.* 11.72.

16. Appian ascribes this action to his general Taxiles who was prominent in the invasion of Greece. Archelaus, another former senior general was with Lucullus.

17. Appian, *Mith.* 11.75, says that 15,000 men, 6,000 horses and a large number of pack animals were captured. Plutarch, *Luc.* 11.3, gives identical information which suggests they used the same source at this point,

although elsewhere they are plainly at odds. There are several towns in Asia Minor named after Apollo, none of the more famous can be the one referred to here. An Apollonia in the Meander valley lies too far south while another Apollonia in Phrygia is too far inland, and a third lay close to Pergamum in the province of Asia.

18. The Romans must have had warships in the region with which to capture Aristonicus yet at the same time were unable to prevent Mithridates' escape. They had lost a fleet at Chalcedon, but that could not have been the entire Roman naval force in Asia Minor.

19. When Lucullus had been Sulla's quaestor he had been sent to various places around the eastern Mediterranean including Syria and Egypt to collect a fleet, A. Keaveny, *Lucullus: A Life* (London 1992) 21–31.

20. This suggests a certain amount of military intelligence at work if this man Marius or Varius was known to be a commander of this particular flotilla.

21. Note the inconsistencies in the Roman Varius or Marius and the rivers Aesepus or Granicus. Plutarch suggests a westward retreat but does not name Lampsacus. Nicomedia seems rather close to Cyzicus as a safe haven for Mithridates but it was on the main route into Pontus.

22. Because of a fall in sea level, Ilium or ancient Troy now lies some kilometres inland, and this harbour, in reality a beaching place, was supposedly the place where the Greeks led by Agamemnon had landed and made camp in their great siege of ten years. Strabo, 13.1.36, describes this '*naustathmos*' as being situated about 12 stades or about 1,400 metres from the city. Appian has Lucullus capture thirteen ships, but Plutarch is less specific stating only that the enemy ships were seen near this harbour.

23. This also shows that the Romans at this point did not control the Hellespont, Lampsacus being at its northern end and Ilium at its southern end.

24. This spot, says Appian, Mith. 11 77, was where the Greek hero Philoctetes had been marooned on his way to the siege of Troy, left behind by his fellow Greeks.

25. Appian mentions subterranean fighting in elaborate and apparently very large tunnels constructed by the invaders and counter tunnelling by defenders, amongst other unusual features of this siege warfare. Amisus was a seaport so it was possible to run a Roman blockade especially if it was confined to the land, but the other cities lay inland. For Themiscyra situated on the River Thermodon and the sieges of this time, see Plutarch, Luc. 14.2; Keaveney (1992) 87–8.

26. Quite what Greeks were doing hiding in a cave close to the Roman camp is left undisclosed by Plutarch. It is possible that these were mercenaries

who had deserted from the Pontic army, but the tale does again look suspiciously contrived to move the narrative along.

27. Plutarch gives the names of the opposing commanders in each instance, Sornatius and Hadrianus the two Romans placed in command of two grain supply columns, Menander, Menemachus and Myron the defeated Pontic leaders, Luc. 17.1. Appian's account may be vague, but it is not necessarily the less accurate.

Chapter 9 (pp. 85–95)

1. Plutarch insists that another sister named Nyasa was captured at Cabira, *Luc.* 18.2.
2. Appian, *Mith.* 12.82, calls him Bacchus, who was sent 'to put the sisters, wives and concubines of the king to death in any way he could. They were stabbed, poisoned and hanged …'
3. The future consul of 54 aged then in his mid-twenties and so likely to have held the rank of military tribune. He was also Lucullus' brother-in-law.
4. Plutarch, *Luc.* 20.3–4, states that the twenty talents fine imposed on the cities of the province by Sulla had, because of exorbitant and probably illegal interest rates, reached 120 talents. Lucullus reduced the interest rates on loans to one percent and forbade irregularities in charging for loans. As a result it is claimed that the debts of the cities were repaid in four years.
5. See further the discussion in Chapter 10.
6. Plutarch's chronology differs quite considerably from Appian at this point. The former has the kings united in friendship prior to Lucullus' invasion of Armenia, Appian only after this had already begun, *Mith.* 12.85.
7. Appian says that a messenger who had brought this unpleasant news to the king had been executed, but such a penalty would surely not have applied to a trusted courtier. However, Plutarch, *Luc.* 22.1–5, does make the point that advisors to these kings lived a dangerous life which could be brought swiftly to an end by the whim of the autocrat. It may also be that Appian believed Tigranes was also not easily accessible if, having wintered in Antioch, he had returned south to the Levant.
8. This weakness in cavalry was not a lesson learned quickly by the Romans. The debacle at Carrhae in 53 BC was similarly caused by inadequate cavalry cover for the army against Parthian attacks. Campaigns against the Parthians in the 30s equally exposed the weakness of the legions against an enemy which liked to employ soldiers on horseback. It was not until the later Roman Empire that cavalry detachments became a fundamental part of the Roman army.

9. Appian, *Mith.* 12.85 provides this immense figure, but Plutarch's total, *Luc.* 26.6, while less also seems completely unrealistic at 150,000 hoplites or heavily armoured infantry, 20,000 archers and slingers, 55,000 cavalry including 17,000 cataphracts.

10. For further details on this battle see Evans (2003) 26–8. The defeat at Arausio ranked alongside those at the Allia (390), the Caudine Forks (321), Lake Trasimene (217), Cannae (215) and Numantia (137) as among the worst thrashings to be inflicted on Roman armies in the history of the state.

11. Plutarch, *Luc.* 28.7–8, refers to Livy, Strabo and a philosopher named as Antiochus among his sources. Strabo was probably a native of Pontus. Livy probably used contemporary sources such as Theophanes of Mytilene. See also Appendix 1.

12. Tigranes had very recently been spectacularly successful in an invasion of Syria, but this perhaps reflects more the inherent weakness of the Seleucid court than his own talent or the efficiency of his armies.

13. For the identity of this commander see the discussion of Broughton (1984) 3.199–200, and that his *cognomen* may have been Barba which would mean that he was active and mentioned in most of Lucullus' operations between 73 and 68.

14. Plutarch, *Luc.* 31.1–2, comments that the harvest was late in these parts because of the cold climate.

15. Appian, *Mith.* 13.88, says that Mithridates, presumably in the thick of the fighting on horseback was wounded in the knee by a stone and nearly lost an eye when hit in the face by an arrow. His action on the battlefield again is highly reminiscent of the personal heroism of Antiochus III.

16. Appian also states such were the fears for Mithridates' health that and as soon as he was able he was lifted up by attendants so that his troops could see that was still alive. When Alexander had been badly wounded in the siege of the Mallians in India, when his life was no longer in danger he had displayed himself to his army from a barge on the Hydraotes river, Arrian, *Anabasis* 6.9–13. It is possible that Mithridates allowed this 'copying' of Alexander's actions, more likely that it became a heroic *topos* inserted into the appropriate places in historical works by ancient writers.

17. Plutarch, *Luc.* 35.1, gives similarly exaggerated totals: 7,000 killed including 150 centurions and 24 tribunes and that the Romans also lost their camp to the enemy. Plutarch and Appian clearly have the same source here, perhaps not Livy, but rather a source seeking to enhance the crisis just before Pompey took command to 'retrieve' the near disaster. Theophanes immediately comes to mind in this context.

18. It was claimed that Artaxata, named after Artaxias, an ancestor of Tigranes who was persuaded to build this city by Hannibal who, it is claimed, came

this way after the defeat of Antiochus III by the Romans in 189, Plut., *Luc.* 31.3, 32.3.

19. On this episode see most recently W.J. Tatum, *The Patrician Tribune: Publius Clodius Pulcher*, Chapel Hill (1999) 44–9. Clodius left Lucullus' camp and joined the staff of the governor of Cilicia, Q. Marcius Rex, another brother-in-law.

Chapter 10 (pp. 97–107)

1. M'. Acilius Glabrio, consul in 67, and proconsul in Asia and Bithynia 67/6.
2. With Pompey's support Gabinius became consul in 58.
3. This was absolutely necessary since many pirate strongholds lay in inlets and not necessarily on the coastal stretches along the sea. Although Pompey had been given extraordinary powers with his command only this clause allowed him a free hand to pursue pirates into provinces governed by other senators. However, this was also seen as a threat to the current status of senatorial governors previously in supreme control of their provincial commands.
4. *Publicani* were Romans of equestrian status who took out licenses to collect the taxes or tribute from the Roman provinces since there was no civilian administration in place to fulfil this important and necessary task. These tax farmers then sent out officials to collect the taxes levying interest on the amounts in order to make a profit from the venture. It was a highly efficient and successful system of private enterprise, even if it was somewhat open to abuse.
5. Metellus Pius was also the pontifex maximus or chief priest of the state's religious cults and would not ordinarily have been allowed such a lengthy absence from his duties. But needs must and the Romans always adapted to novel situations and regarded nothing as set in stone.
6. For Marius' appointment to the command in Numidia superseding Q. Caecilius Metellus Numidicius see Evans (1994) 68–78.
7. He retained his powers under the Gabinian law of 67, and the *lex Manilia* added the provinces of Bithynia and Cilicia and generally the whole of Asia Minor to his command. The wide ranging *imperium* was on a larger scale than any assigned before in the state's history, but then the empire had been never more extensive.
8. For Pompey's dislike of Lucullus see Plutarch, *Pomp.* 30. Lucullus had been close to Sulla, certainly closer than Pompey seems to have been. Yet it was Pompey's early military triumphs which might have been a source of envy for those like Lucullus, who pursued a much more conventional career, although he had also been highly successful in his youth, rather

than the other way around. Later when Pompey was in Spain he complained of a lack of supplies from Rome and he may have regarded Lucullus who was consul in 74 as impeding a successful outcome of that war.

9. Q. Marcius Rex was governor of Cilicia in 66, while M'. Acilius Glabrio was proconsul of Asia in the same year, Broughton (1984) 3.2–3. Neither figure was friendly or supportive towards Lucullus.

10. Night attacks were rare but are recorded in the literature, the most famous, recorded by Thucydides, 7.43–5, being that of Demosthenes against the western fortifications of Syracuse across the plateau of Epipolai in August 413. His troops quickly became lost and were attacked by the defenders who knew the ground so much better, and the Athenians suffered heavy casualties in a chaotic retreat back down to their camp. Alexander the Great was advised by Parmenio to make a night attack on the Persians at Gaugamela in 331 to reduce the possible disadvantage of the Greek numerical inferiority. Naturally he refused, but word must have got about since the Persians spent the night under arms expecting an attack, and so were tired and hungry when Alexander led out his forces in the morning well rested and fed.

11. Appian, *Mith.* 15.100, has much the same information but appears to place the battle inside Pontus and does not mention a river crossing or a battle at night. He also has Mithridates retreat to a fortress named as Sinorega and from there into Colchis, but with a more substantial force, than that granted to him by Plutarch. This may well account for the fact that the Colchians accepted his presence without opposition.

12. Lucius Afranius was later consul in 61. Pompey always rewarded his friends.

13. Appian, *Mith.* 15.103, has essentially the same information but places the defeat of the local tribes prior to the invasion and occupation of Armenia, including the discovery of women warriors who, it is claimed, might have been the legendary Amazons. Plutarch places the discovery of 'Amazon' fighters after the battle with Cosis and the Albanians. Both writers digress about the origin and historicity of the Amazons, a favourite topic for historians who tackled events in this region, supposedly the home of this solely female tribe. This Servilius was probably P. Servilius Vatia, consul in 47 and quaestor perhaps in 61 or more likely earlier if he was with Pompey in a position of some importance in 66/5, Broughton (1984) 3.196.

14. Appian states that the younger Tigranes was exhibited at Pompey's triumph in 61 and executed afterwards which implies more than just pique at Pompey's arrangements. If accurate this information suggests that Tigranes had been foiled in some sort of plotting.

15. Appian says, *Mith.* 16.107–8, that the severity of the exactions was done in his name by unscrupulous ministers while he himself was ill with ulcers to his face. He did not show himself in public while this unattractive infection lasted and was attended apparently by just three eunuchs. It does seem unlikely however that such a disease would have also prevented this particularly energetic king from carrying out his duties.
16. Along with the younger Tigranes they are mentioned by Appian, *Mith.* 17.117, as being present in Rome in Pompey's triumph in 61.
17. Plutarch, *Pomp.* 41.3, has Pompey in Petra when news of Mithridates' suicide arrived and returning to Amisus to receive the king's body, which was sent from there to Sinope. On Petra, see also the final chapter.

Chapter 11 (pp. 109–112)

1. The brother of the poet Catullus seems to have served with Pompey and died in the Troad probably from some sickness.
2. Arbela was the nearest town to Gaugamela, the site of Alexander's victory over Darius III in 331 BC.
3. For a more detailed discussion see R. Seager, *Pompey: A Political Biography* (Oxford 1979) 50–5.

Select Bibliography

Ancient Sources

Appian, *The Syrian Wars* and *The Mithridatic Wars*, in *Appian's Roman History*, Volume 2 (The Loeb Classical Library: Harvard 1912).

Livy: Rome and the Mediterranean, trans. H. Bettenson (Penguin: Harmondsworth 1976).

Memnon, *History of Heracleia*, trans. Andrew Smith (© attalus.org).

Plutarch's Lives, Volume 2, trans. B. Perrin (The Loeb Classical Library: Harvard 1914).

Plutarch, *Makers of Rome: Nines Lives by Plutarch*, trans. I. Scott-Kilvert (Penguin: Harmondsworth 1965).

Plutarch, *Fall of the Roman Republic*, trans. R. Warner (Penguin: Harmondsworth 1958).

Polybius, *The Histories*, Six Volumes, trans. W.R. Paton (The Loeb Classical Library: Harvard 1922–26).

Polybius, *The Rise of the Roman Empire*, trans. I. Scott-Kilvert (Penguin: Harmondsworth 1979).

Modern Works

Astin, A.E., *Cato the Censor* (Oxford 1978).

Badian, E., *Roman Imperialism in the Late Republic* (Ithaca 1981).

Bevan, E.R., *The House of Seleucus* (London 1902).

Bosworth, A.B., *The Legacy of Alexander: Politics, Warfare, and Propaganda under the Successors* (Oxford 2002).

Briscoe, J., *A Commentary on Livy Books XXXI–XXXIII* (Oxford 1973).

Briscoe, J., *A Commentary on Livy Books XXXIV–XXXVII* (Oxford 1981).

Broughton, T.R.S., 'Stratoniceia and Aristonicus', *Classical Philology* 29 (1934) 252–254.

Broughton, T.R.S., *The Magistrates of the Roman Republic*, Volumes 1 and 2 (New York 1951-52).

Broughton, T.R.S., *The Magistrates of the Roman Republic*, Volume 3 (Atlanta 1984).

Crawford, M.H., *The Roman Republic* (London 1978).

Ekstein, A.M., *Rome Enters the Greek east: From Anarchy to Hierarchy in the Hellenistic Mediterranean, 230–170 BC* (Oxford 2008).

Erskine, A., *Troy between Greece and Rome* (Oxford 2001).

Evans, R.J., 'The Moneyership of Marcus Lepidus Triumvir', *Acta Classica* 33 (1990) 103–108.

Evans, R.J., *A Short History of Rome* (Cape Town 1991).

Evans, R.J., *Gaius Marius: A Political Biography* (Pretoria 1994).

Evans, R.J., *Questioning Reputations: Essays on Nine Roman Republican Politicians* (Pretoria 2003).

Evans, R.J., *A History of Pergamum: Beyond Hellenistic Kingship* (London 2012).

Evans, R.J., *Fields of Death: Retracing Ancient Battlefields* (Barnsley 2013).

Evans, R.J., *Fields of Battle: Retracing Ancient Battlefields* (Barnsley 2015).

Errington, R.M., 'Rome and Greece to 205 B.C.', in *The Cambridge Ancient History* Volume 8, 85–94 (Cambridge 1989).

Grainger, J.D., *The Roman War of Antiochos the Great* (Leiden 2002).

Gruen, E.S., *The Hellenistic World and the Coming of Rome* (Berkeley 1986).

Habicht, C, 'The Seleucids and their Rivals' in *The Cambridge Ancient History* Volume 8, 324–387 (Cambridge 1989).

Hackett, General Sir John (ed.), *Warfare in the Ancient World* (London 1989).

Hammond N.G.L. & H.H. Scullard (eds.), *The Oxford Classical Dictionary* (Second Edition) (Oxford 1970).

Harris, W.V., *War and Imperialism in Republican Rome, 327–70 BC* (Oxford 1992).

Keaveney, A., 'Studies in the *Dominatio Sullae*', *Klio* 65 (1983) 185–208.

Keaveney, A., *Lucullus: A Life* (London 1992).

Lampela, A., *Rome and the Ptolemies of Egypt* (Helsinki 1998).

Leach, J., *Pompey the Great* (London 1978).

Lewis, N. & Reinhold, M., *Roman Civilisation: Sourcebook 1: The Republic* (Columbia 1966).

Rosenstein N. & R. Morstein-Marx (eds.), *A Companion to the Roman Republic* (Oxford 2006).

Sabin, P., *Lost Battles: Reconstructing the Great Clashes of the Ancient World* (London 2007).

Scullard, H.H., *Roman Politics 220–150 B.C.* (Oxford 1973).

Scullard, H.H., *From the Gracchi to Nero: A History of Rome 133 BC to AD 68* (London 1982).

Seager, R., *Pompey: A Political Biography* (Oxford 1979).

Sherwin-White, S & Kuhrt A., *From Samarkand to Sardis* (London 1993).

Shipley, G., Vanderspoel, J., Mattingly, D., Foxhall, L., (eds.), *The Cambridge Dictionary of Classical Civilisation* (Cambridge 2008).

Sidkey, H., *The Greek Kingdom of Bactria* (New York 2000).

Talbert, R.J.A., *Atlas of Classical History* (London 1985).

Tatum, W.J., *The Patrician Tribune: Publius Clodius Pulcher* (Chapel Hill 1999).

Walbank, F.W., *A Historical Commentary on Polybius*, Volume 1: Commentary on Books I–VI (Oxford 1957).

Weigel, R.D., *Lepidus the Tarnished Triumvir* (London 1992).

Wiseman, T.P., *The Myths of Rome* (Exeter 2004).

Index

Theophanes of Mytilene, 99, 101–3, 137
    n. 11 & 17
Theophilus of Paphlagonia, 55
Thermodon River, 102, 135 n. 25
Thermopylae (battle at), 29, 32–4, 44, 114,
    131 n. 20
Thespiae, 33
Thessaly, 2, 31–2, 57, 61
Third Macedonian War (170–168), 3
Third Punic War (149–146), 3, 50
Thoas (Aetolian leader), 29, 45
Thrace, 8, 11, 20, 25–6, 34–5, 37, 57, 59,
    63, 74, 90, 101
Thucydides (Greek historian), 139 n. 10
Thurium ('cone-shaped hill'), 60–1
Thyateira, 38, 44, 65
Tigranes I ('the Great,' king of Armenia,
    100–56), 24, 71, 80–1, 86–94, 101, 103,
    109–10
Tigranes (son of Tigranes I), 90, 103, 109,
    139 n. 14
Tigranocerta, 24, 71, 86–92, 103
Tigris River, xii, 89, 110
Tilphossium (Mt), 61
Timaeus of Tauromenion (Greek historian),
    119 n. 3
Timotheus (physician to Mithridates), 94
Tortuga, 52
Tralles, 40–1, 44–5, 55
Trapezus, 71
Triarii, 40
Troad, 19, 63, 65, 67, 77, 79

Troy (Ilium), 6, 7, 79, 109, 135 n. 22
Trypho (general of Mithridates VI), 104
Tullius Cicero, M. (consul 63), xi, 52;
    speech *pro Murena* 65, 99, 115
Turkey, 19
Tyre, 29, 74–5
Tyrrenhian Sea ('Mare Nostrum'), 1, 98

Utica, 3

Valerius Antias (Roman historian) 123 n. 4
Valerius Flaccus, L. (consul 86), 58, 62–3,
    65
Valerius Triarius, C. (legate of Lucullus),
    78, 93–5
Varius, M., 78–9, 134 n. 7
Vitellius (Roman emperor), 115

Xenophon (Greek historian), 24
Xerxes (Persian king), 33
Xerxes (son of Mithridates VI), 104
Xiphares (son of Mithridates VI), 104

Zama (battle of), 3, 26, 99
Zeno (Greek historian), 17
Zeus, 20, 21; as Zeus Stratius 69
Zeuxis (general of Antiochus III), 41, 44